THE UPSET BOOK

A GUIDE FOR DEALING WITH UPSET PEOPLE

Pennie Myers & Don Nance
The Wichita State University

Academic Publications
Notre Dame, Indiana

Cover design by Melissa Porter

The Upset Book
is published by
Academic Publications
Box 478, South Bend, IN 46556-0609

**Library of Congress Cataloging in
Publication Data**

ISBN 0-937647-01-2

CONTENTS

Acknowledgments

Chapter 1 Introduction   1

Chapter 2 Channels of Communication   17

Chapter 3 A Conceptual Framework For   44
Dealing With Upset Persons

Chapter 4 Making Positive Contact   59

Chapter 5 Dealing with Upset People   82

Chapter 6 Dealing with Angry People   133

Chapter 7 Dealing with Loss   171

Chapter 8 Putting it all Together   208

References and reading   219

About the Authors

Acknowledgments

A special thank you to our many clients, workshop participants, friends and family members who, through the years, have shared a myriad of personal experiences with us thereby enabling us to develop *The Upset Book*. It is to all of them that this book is dedicated.

The support of our professional colleagues is especially appreciated not only for all the consultative editing advice which they provided, but also for tolerating us during some of our more difficult moments. Throughout the writing process, all of us learned that the ideas in *The Upset Book* do indeed work.

CHAPTER ONE
INTRODUCTION

The woman who entered our office looked considerably older than thirty-five, the age which appeared on her client file. She sank into a chair and announced that she wasn't sure whether she needed work-related consultation or marital counseling. Peggy was the customer service representative for a large utility company. Most of her day was spent coping with upset consumers. She was exhausted by her daily contact with angry people who had gripes against the company. Many of her work days ended unhappily. Either she inappropriately exploded at a customer or she stalked home and played "kick the dog" with members of her family — sometimes both. Peggy was fearful of losing her job. She worried about her relationship with her family. A friend of Peggy's suggested she call us for some help dealing with upset people. Improving her people skills, she hoped, would also improve her job and her family situation.

Peggy's problem is a problem for all of us. No one escapes dealing with upset people. No one escapes feeling upset. Upset people are just ordinary folks whose irritation, anger, sadness, or grief has been activated. Friends, family members, and colleagues in the workplace are sometimes upset persons. Nice people, quiet people, easy-going people, slow to anger people all experience feelings of upset at times. Each of us has been both an upset person and the one who has had to deal with others who are upset.

This book presents a systematic plan for dealing with upset people. We anticipate that when you finish the book you'll be able to make three statements about yourself when it comes to dealing with upset people:

"I already have some of the attitudes and behaviors that help in dealing with upset people." (Each of us has already acquired many skills related to dealing with upset persons. We hope you will take time to praise and appreciate your successes.)

"I learned some new ways to prevent and handle upset in others." (We can only do what we know how to do. The more behaviors we know how to use, the more opportunity we have to succeed. New skills are developed through learning and practicing.)

"I have learned some new ways of thinking about, organizing, and using principles related to upset persons." (Understanding what causes upset, understanding what happens to *us* when we are confronted with an upset person, and understanding why some strategies work better than others when dealing with upset people improves our chances for success when it comes to dealing with upset persons.)

As you read this book, think about the upset people you've had to deal with and imagine yourself replaying some of the scenes with the attitudes and behaviors described. Each of us knows at least one or two persons who are going to remain upset no matter what we say or do. Nothing could help to reduce their upset. These people are atypical and in the minority. Allow yourself to focus on the majority of people with whom the principles for dealing with upset people outlined in this book will work.

The Upset Book is rooted in the belief that much of the upset that we encounter can be prevented by utilizing positive contact skills with people. Therefore, our book addresses how to prevent upset in people who initially are not upset at all. Of course, in addition to "prevention" skills, we also need "curative" skills for people who are already upset. Our formulas for dealing with complaints, anger, grief, and other difficult situations grow and develop in the fertile soil of several well-accepted theories and find fruition in the basics of good communication.

The chapters in *The Upset Book* are organized in

the following way. Chapter Two describes the seven channels of communication. These channels of communication will serve as our communication building blocks for dealing with upset people. Chapter Three presents ideas from Transactional Analysis and Rational Emotive Therapy. These ideas help to explain some of the causes of upset. They also help us to understand which strategies are most likely to succeed in dealing with upset in ourselves and others. Making positive contact is the subject of Chapter Four. Positive contact is one of the easiest ways to prevent upset in others. Preventing upset means we have fewer upset people to handle. Chapter Five provides a formula for handling upset people and addresses some of the common problems encountered in dealing with upset in others. How to handle angry people is the subject of Chapter Six, which discusses the causes of anger and includes a formula for handling angry people and specific techniques for dealing with extreme anger. Chapter Seven describes methods for dealing with people who have experienced a loss or some unwanted change in their lives. Upset can be the result of many kinds of loss, including the death of a loved one, loss of a job, divorce, children leaving home to start their adult lives, the loss of health, or the aging process. The final chapter summarizes the theory and practice of handling upset persons.

Within some of the following chapters are skill-building activities related to the discussion in that particular chapter. The way to improve at something is through practice. Athletes know this and spend many hours perfecting their skills. Rather than attempt to learn new skills at the game, they do so in practice situations. We hope you will consider the activities within various sections of the book as opportunities for practice prior to the game. Please use them as suggested activities from which you can create additional ways for handling upset persons. Also, keep in mind that once the basics of a new skill are learned, players must go out in the field to gain experience. Don't expect to compete flawlessly. Expect only improved performance with each attempt. Don't be afraid to use what you are learning and don't be too hard on yourself. You're bound to miss a ball now and then.

Before reading any further, take a few minutes to complete the Dealing with Upset People Profile. We hope that by taking this profile, you will begin thinking about those attitudes and behaviors that contribute to the upset of other people. The profile may also help you begin to understand what it is that upsets *you* when you are faced with a complaining, angry or depressed person. Some of the principles for dealing with upset people that we will be discussing throughout the book are previewed in the profile. You may find it helpful to relate specific situations that you have encountered to each of the questions. Our hope is that the profile will get you into the mood for mastering the art of dealing with people who are upset. In Chapter Eight, we will review the profile and discuss each of the statements in it.

DEALING WITH UPSET PEOPLE PROFILE

Please rate each of the following twelve statements by assigning it the number on the five-point scale that most closely matches how you see yourself.

almost never	infre- quently	some- times	usually	almost always
5	4	3	2	1

1) I have trouble listening to people because there are no new complaints— just the same old ones replayed over and over again. ___

2) I am afraid to show concern for other people's problems for fear they will expect me to do something.   ___

3) My day is made or ruined by the moods of people around me.   ___

4) I try to convince other people by talking a lot and using logical arguments.   ___

5) I talk about myself a lot.   ___

6) I hate to be interrupted by people when I'm in the middle of working on something.   ___

7) I am uncomfortable when I don't know the answer to a question I am asked or when I don't know what to say to an upset person.   ___

8) I have trouble listening to someone when I already know I won't be able to find a solution to their problem.   ___

9) I feel that other people's upset is personally directed at me.   ___

10) I feel good when I've remained rational, even if the other person remains upset.   ___

11) I don't like to refer an upset person because it says I am not being helpful enough.   ___

12) I feel frustrated when I don't have the power to help someone resolve their problem.   ___

TOTAL SCORE   ___

Add your individual item scores for a total score. Your score can range from 12 to 60. The higher your score, the more successful you are likely to be at handling upset persons. Scores above 42 suggest above-average attitudes and skills related to handling people. If you score below 36, you probably need to improve some of your attitudes and behaviors in order to deal successfully with people. We hope that by the time you have read *The Upset Book* and practiced the behaviors outlined throughout it, your Dealing with Upset Persons Profile score will be at an above-average level and you will feel more comfortable about handling upset situations. We recommend retaking the profile for self-assessment purposes after you have finished the book.

SIX PRINCIPLES FOR DEALING WITH UPSET PERSONS

Self-Esteem

Six principles form the foundation for handling upset persons. The first principle states: **It is important to interact with others in such a way that no-one's self-esteem is damaged.** In dealing with upset people, we can become upset by our own behavior as well as by the behavior of the upset person. This is most likely to happen if we have behaved inappropriately — perhaps yelling back, or not being as helpful as we might have been. The goal in handling others who are upset is to have all those who participated in the situation feel good about the way in which they conducted themselves. Everyone should be able to feel proud of his or her own behavior. No one should need to avoid further contact due to anger or embarrassment.

Not long ago, after presenting this material to the sales force of a large midwestern manufacturing company, one of the employees described a person with whom she had had many upsetting phone conversations. She felt hopeless about ever developing a satisfactory business relationship with this person. After attending our Dealing with Upset Persons Seminar, she reluctantly decided to give some of the "stuff" a try. To her surprise, things improved. Her job became more pleasant and she felt good about her ability to cope with a difficult person.

It helps when, at the end of the day, you feel you handled yourself and others well. This reduces the probability of catching and spreading the "upset person syndrome." Being irritable at the end of a difficult work day is unlikely to improve the situation. We only spread our upset to our loved ones.

The Most Important Person

Do you have a favorite store? What about the business establishment you vowed never again to do business with? Is there a friend with whom you consistently enjoy spending time? Are your preferences about where to trade, shop, and eat based on particular people? If so, you can readily get a sense of the second principle for dealing with upset persons. The second principle states: **The most important person in any setting is the person with whom you have contact.** The impact of the contact person is immediate. Customers, clients, or patients are as frequently won or lost by receptionists, salespeople, and service representatives as they are by management policies, products, or professionals. I (Pennie) value good medical care. I liked my doctor and respected her competence. However, I changed family physicians based on frequent difficulties with the physician's receptionist. I (Don) enjoy weekend breakfasts at a particular restaurant because one of the waiters is so pleasant and competent — not because the eggs are noticeably superior.

The principle of the *Most Important Person* means that each of us has the power to affect the well-being of those around us. Our impact is strong and immediate. The manner in which we handle our child who is upset by a school problem can have a greater effect on our child's response to that problem than do teachers, principals, and school policy. In our work settings and as parents, spouses, friends, and lovers, we are more important than we sometimes feel. How each of us handles other people *can* make a significant difference because we are the *most important person* to those with whom we interact.

Being in Charge of Yourself

A third principle for dealing with upset persons states: **People can be in charge of their own behavior in ways that help them successfully manage the behavior of others.** We *can* have an impact on what happens in our dealings with other people. If we approach other people with a smile, they smile back because they expect to have a pleasant interaction with us. On the other hand, if we approach others with an angry facial expression or clenched fists, they prepare themselves for self-protection. How we approach other people influences how they respond to us. It is possible through self-mastery to have mostly positive relationships with other people. We can use our own behavior to elicit the behaviors we want from other people.

A discouraged repairman, in talking about his customers, said: "If they're nice to me, I'm nice to them and if they're not nice to me, I'm not nice to them." "Do you mean that even if you've been driving down the road singing and feeling great, a growling customer can change your entire mood and make you feel lousy?" we asked. "Yup," he replied.

How powerless people can permit themselves to be when they allow others to control their moods so easily! Being in charge of yourself encourages the successful handling of upset persons.

Against the Natural Tendency

Closely related to the principle of being in charge of yourself is a fourth principle for dealing with upset persons which states: **Effective dealing with upset persons often requires us to go against our natural tendencies.** This principle, like the principle of being in charge of yourself, is rooted in the idea that "like begets like." The natural tendency when someone smiles at us is to smile back. When approached with anger, our impulse is to be angry in return. Therefore, to handle upset persons, we must sometimes resist our natural tendency to match the upset person's behavior. Angry friends who call with a complaint about the way in which we treated them are likely to escalate their anger if we get angry in return. They are more likely to respond positively if we are pleasant. Fighting the natural tendency to respond in kind is no easy task! It *is* possible to learn to control instinctive behavior in favor of self-control. The ideas and suggestions throughout this book are aimed at helping the reader to control natural tendencies that are ineffective in handling upset persons. Although this is hard work, the benefits are great!

Primary and Secondary Upset

The fifth principle in dealing with upset persons states: **Primary upset needs to be managed so that it will not escalate into secondary upset.** Secondary upset is the upset that results from not having our initial complaints handled appropriately. A consumer story illustrates the principle of primary versus secondary upset.

> When my (Pennie's) daughter was three years old her grandmother bought her a bathrobe for her birthday. Grandmother thought she'd purchased a Size 4. When the box was opened, the robe was a Size 6. A hurried trip was made to exchange the robe for the correct size. At that point grandmother, mother, and daughter had primary upset — a touch of annoyance at having purchased the wrong

size. After dealing with the salesperson, the primary upset escalated into secondary upset. We became disturbed and upset by the way in which we were treated. The salesperson noticed a missing button on the robe. She said, "I think you are returning used merchandise." Her accusations escalated and our upset increased. She refused to exchange the robe. Suffice it to say that in the last twenty-two years no-one in our family has purchased anything from this particular children's store. The salesperson cost the store dearly by her poor handling of a simple complaint.

Secondary upset can be easily observed in our personal relationships. Disagreements can turn into fights because a loved one expressed a minor complaint that was ignored or debated. The focus of the upset switches from the initial complaint to the response. Secondary upset is costly. Lost sales or impaired relationships are expensive to the parties involved. The importance of preventing secondary upset cannot be overemphasized. Helpful prevention skills of making positive contact with people and of handling complaints will be discussed in later chapters.

Soft to Hard

The last principle in dealing with upset persons is described as: **Working from "soft to hard."** Working from soft to hard means that we use the softest behaviors possible in dealing with other people. Security guards and police dogs are unnecessary when an understanding ear will do as well or better. An admonishing look may be all that is necessary to quiet a noisy child. "I'm sorry you had a bad day" has helped calm many an upset spouse or friend. Kind, courteous, and quick responses help to reduce most people's upset. Save your strongest measures for those situations that require more drastic controlling strategies. It makes more sense to move from soft to hard than to start out hard and have no place to go. Working soft to hard is useful for parents. Children of parents who yell all the time have simply learned to turn down their parents' volume. When our toddler runs out into the street, we want to reprimand sternly and in a no-nonsense manner. If it takes a raised voice and a light swat on the behind to let the child know how serious we are, then that is what we do. But the toddler who needs a reminder to pick up his or her toys at the end of the day doesn't need the first reminder to involve raised voices or spankings. The most successful parents are those who match the level of the reprimand to the level of the child's misbehavior. Working soft to hard saves everyone unnecessary wear and tear.

By now you have completed your Dealing With Upset Persons Profile and have an understanding of the principles involved in handling people who are upset. It is time to roll up our sleeves and get busy. The sooner you have improved your attitudes toward and skills for handling upset people, the sooner you can enjoy the wonderful feelings of success. As you turn to Chapter Two, be prepared to focus your attention on the nuts and bolts of how people talk to one another.

CHAPTER TWO
CHANNELS OF COMMUNICATION

The woman behind the chest-high counter at the travel club perfunctorily asked, "How can I help you?" We requested several local maps and the tour guide book for the area. As she gathered the requested materials, she mumbled and grumbled to herself and in handing us the tour book announced in an irritated tone, "You should get tour books at your local chapter office." Slamming things around on her desk, she filled out a club exchange receipt and presented it mechanically for a signature. The message she was communicating came through loud and clear and bore little resemblance to her initial suggestion of wanting to be helpful.

Good communication is important for preventing and managing upset in people. The purpose of this chapter is to describe the basic components of communication. These components will be used as building blocks in the formulas described in subsequent chapters. We need a common frame of reference and language for understanding what is happening in the communication process. The seven channels of communication described in this chapter are useful conceptual models for understanding the communication process at a *behavioral* level. We will look at two additional models for understanding the communication process at a *psychological* level in Chapter Three.

THE COMMUNICATION PROCESS

Every time we engage in even the briefest interaction with someone, a very complex process of communication is taking place. We are so accustomed to the process, that often we are totally unaware of its complexity. This is not unlike trying to remember all the individual tasks that one must master before being able to drive an automobile safely. When we are learning to drive, we are cognizant of each individual element. In fact, it is only after we have attained proficiency in the overall task that we lose sight of and stop paying attention to the smaller components. If, however, we suddenly became accident prone, we would need to return to dissecting what we were doing around each element of driving. We would also need to examine our vehicle in detail to see what problems it might be having and how we could correct them. Preventative and repairative maintenance are crucial. The relationship between the driver and the car is an interactive one.

So, too, the communication process is an interactive one between the sender and the receiver. We are called upon countless times every day to utilize our own channels of communication in sending messages and to attend to other people's channels in order to decipher the messages sent to us. Good communicators send the same message on all channels. Good communicators are also skilled at scanning the senders' channels.

The following self-assessment tool has no right or wrong answers. You need only assess yourself as to current skill level on a number of communication dimensions. The Communication Questionaire can also be a useful tool for gathering feedback from others about their perceptions of you as a communicator. You might find it helpful to ask a boss, a coworker, a supervisee, a friend, or a family member to fill out the communication questionaire about you.

INTERPERSONAL COMMUNICATION INVENTORY

Please rate yourself by placing a check mark in he column which most fits your assessment of your current behavior on each item.

	Doing Well	Doing All Right	Need To Do Less	Need to Do More
Being concise and getting to the point	___	___	___	___
Being forceful and definite rather than hesitant and apologetic when necessary	___	___	___	___
Being specific and giving examples in order to make communication more clear	___	___	___	___
Giving an overview when details are not necessary	___	___	___	___
Letting others know when I do not understand something they have said	___	___	___	___
Letting others know when I like something they have said or done	___	___	___	___
Letting others know when I disagree with them	___	___	___	___
Letting others know when I think they have become irrelevant	___	___	___	___
Letting others know when I am getting irritated or angry	___	___	___	___
Letting others know when I feel hurt by something they have said or done	___	___	___	___
Listening to understand rather than preparing my next remark	___	___	___	___

	Doing Well	Doing All Right	Need To Do Less	Need to Do More
Helping others participate in a conversation or in a discussion	—	—	—	—
Checking to make sure I understand what others are saying	—	—	—	—
Summarizing points of disagreement and agreement	—	—	—	—
Asking questions that get information	—	—	—	—
Checking out with others what I think they are feeling	—	—	—	—
Responding to a person who is upset in a way that does not ignore his/her feelings	—	—	—	—
Responding to a person who is expressing closeness	—	—	—	—
Talking in group discussions	—	—	—	—
Being aware when I am coping with my own feelings	—	—	—	—
Getting feedback from others	—	—	—	—

	Doing Well	Doing All Right	Need To Do Less	Need to Do More
Being able to stand silence	__	__	__	__
Being able to stand conflict	__	__	__	__
Accepting help from others	__	__	__	__
Offering help to others	__	__	__	__
Giving in to others	__	__	__	__
Asserting myself	__	__	__	__
Backing up others when necessary	__	__	__	__

Now that you have feedback from yourself and perhaps others on your communication skills, select three items that you or others think you do well. Enjoy feeling good about these skills. Also select three items on which you would like to improve. As you continue reading the book, utilize the skill-building exercises in order to improve in your targeted areas.

SEVEN CHANNELS OF COMMUNICATION

Anytime people are communicating, they are doing so in many different ways. We are labeling the different ways through which people communicate the *channels of communication.* These seven channels form the basic building blocks of communication.

Channel One: Language
Word choice and labels

The first chanel of communication is the language channel. The "what" of our message is transmitted on this channel through the words we choose and the way we string them together. It is easy to recognize that if two people speak different languages, it is difficult, perhaps impossible, for them to communicate. Even within languages, miscommunication easily occurs when words have different meanings to different people. The travel club woman described at the beginning of this chapter said, "How can I help you?" Those words were translated literally by the traveler while apparently meaning, "I hope you won't need much or be any trouble" to the travel guide. Word choice and labels are important aspects of Channel One. What something or someone is labeled has significant impact on how a message is received. The word choice in the following messages from parent to child are what distinguishes them and what determines the child's potential response.

"You're such a slob. Clean up your room."

"Please get your room cleaned up by dinner time."

Word choice in the second message does a clearer job of labeling the problem as residing in the messy room rather than in the child.

The subtleties of word choice sometimes escape us because words that are red flags for others may not be so for us. Pejorative words may only be pejorative to the receiver. The civil rights and women's consciousness-raising movements of the 1960s and 1970s sensitized us to the effect words like "girl" and "boy" have on those that are so labeled. The choice of "Miss," "Mrs," or "Ms," for example, often carry significant meaning.

Upset people usually select words that reflect their feelings. Large numbers and imperatives pepper their speech. Phrases like "this is the hundredth time," "you never," "you always," "you have to," "you must" indicate that someone is upset.

Jargon

Occupational groups, social groups, and family groups all have in-group jargon that provides useful shorthand for the members. The problem, however, usually lies in the fact that non-group members don't speak the same language. A critical aspect of word choice is remembering not to use *your* group's jargon with non-group members. Violation of this rule can provoke upset in others and certainly is not useful in defusing anger or grief in already upset persons. For example, clients should be directed to "please complete this application form for assistance with your problem" as opposed to "we'll need to have your RBS 222 on file before we can help you." Similarly, the new babysitter you hire may need to be told specific words your children use related to food, playthings, bathroom habits, etc. Otherwise "need t-t" may be valueless jibberish to the sitter who rushes Johnny to the bathroom when he was requesting tinkertoys or tasty-treats.

Written Communication

A final word about the language channel. Channel One is the only channel available to us for written communication. When we are writing, we have no way to soften a blow or clarify a point with our tone or expression. This means that word choice is particularly critical in letters, memos, notes, reports, etc.

Certainly when writing important messages, it might be a good idea to have someone unfamiliar with the message read or edit it for meaning and interpretation. When you are rereading your own written material, be sure to put yourself in the potential reader's shoes. If you have an option other than a letter or memo for sending messages, you might consider other alternatives.

In summary, Channel One is the backbone of our communication. Word choice, labels, and jargon can assist or impede communication. This channel is particularly sensitive in written communication. Receivers are affected by what they hear while senders select words that reflect their feelings.

Channel Two: Manner

The second channel of communication is the manner channel. Just as Channel One is the "what" of communication, Channel Two is the "how." Tone of voice, clarity, intonation, and pace determine the way messages are transmitted. The words we choose are important, but in oral communication, how we vocalize the words becomes a critical variable. In fact, if Channels One and Two are not congruent, receivers always believe Channel Two over Channel One. Our travel person's manner took precedence over her initial helpful greeting. As senders, good communicators make sure that Channels One and Two are sending the same message.

Channel Two and feelings

Channel Two tells us a lot about the feeling state (Channel Four) of others. People who are upset often send messages about their upset by "how" they communicate. Any exaggeration of tone, clarity, intonation, or pace is what we observe. People who speak too fast or too slow; people who enunciate too clearly or very little; people who speak too softly or very loudly are sending cues that something is amiss. Changes on the manner channel are also significant indicators about feelings. As people get more upset, their pace, tone, clarity, and inflection change.

Telephone contact

Telephone contact uses Channels One and Two. The telephone blocks visual clues. Therefore, because most of us use the telephone regularly, we need to be aware of the impact of Channel Two on our communication. We need to substitute verbal behaviors for behaviors that can't be seen over the phone.

A church secretary was well regarded and considered personable and helpful by most of the congregants with whom she worked. However, there were occasional complaints from individuals who had never met her prior to a phone conversation. In analyzing the problem, it became clear that her voice had a flat quality which was interpreted as anger or disinterest. In face-to-face contact her warmth transcended her voice quality because of her smiles, facial expression and gestures (Channel Three). Voice training using audio tapes as feedback was very helpful.

In summary, Channel Two has a great impact on oral communication. On the telephone, visual cues are missing and therefore Channels One and Two are our only transmitters. Upset persons often use Channel Two to express the magnitude of their feelings. As a receiver it is important to scan Channel Two for indications of how others are feeling. As a sender, it is important to match Channels One and Two to make sure you are heard correctly.

Channel Three: Body Language

The third channel of communication is body language. Facial expression, eye contact, gestures, and posture make up Channel Three. If Channel One is what we say, and Channel Two is how we say it vocally, then Channel Three is how we say it visually. Smiles and tears tell us a lot about each other. Clenched fists cue us into the other person's anger or anxiety. In face-to-face contact we utilize the first three channels to get a reading of the other person's emotional state. Like Channel Two, Channel Three is often a better indicator of how someone is feeling than is Channel One. Channels Two and Three together are the clearest yardsticks of emotion. Sending the same message on all three channels is what we strive for as good communicators. Being able to discern the message on Channels Two and Three is the sign of a good listener.

Changes in body language

Reading another person's body language, while important, can also be overdone. Sometimes, people cross their arms because they don't know what else to do with them. It might be a mistake to interpret these gestures as meaning the person is "closed" to communicating with us or is going to be "a tough nut to crack." What is sometimes significant is a noticeable change or shift in a person's body language.

Mary made an appointment for vocational testing and counseling. She appeared friendly and relaxed with the counselor while discussing her former employment history, skills, interests, and hobbies. A question about her husband's vocation, however, caused Mary to shift uncomfortably in her chair. She began twisting her wedding band, clearing her throat, and stuttering slightly. The counselor noticing this, learned through questions that Mary's husband was planning divorce. A pending divorce necessitated that Mary prepare for a job as soon as possible. Reading Channel Two and Channel Three helped the counselor gain difficult to talk about personal information which was pertinent for good career planning for the client.

All of us can gather and utilize valuable information about others' feelings through observation. If we scan Channel Three, most of us find we can predict the moods of loved ones and friends — sometimes by their footsteps and posture alone. Interestingly, one of the things we are aware of as we write this book is the difficulty of describing Channels Two and Three when the written word, Channel One, is the only tool at our disposal. When presenting this information in seminar form, we can demonstrate Channels Two and Three by using them. To have only one channel on which to communicate is limiting.

In summary, Channel Three, body language helps us to read messages from others through visual cues. People tell us a lot about what they are thinking and feeling through facial expressions, gestures, and postures.   In addition to taking an overall reading of ourselves and others in interactions, it is essential to observe changes in body language and to consider them a barometer of changes in feeling.

Channel Four: Feelings

The fourth channel of communication is the feeling channel.   Feelings get communicated through Channels One, Two, and Three.   In dealing with upset persons, it is critical to understand and respond to the feelings of others.   More will be said about this in Chapters Five, Six, and Seven,   when we describe methods for dealing with   upset persons, angry persons,   and people experiencing a loss.

Static

Unattended feelings represent static on the channels.   When there is a lot of static on any receiver (TV, radio, C.B., or two-way) it is impossible for messages to get through.   This is certainly the case in interpersonal communication.   "Noise" from feelings blocks the messages.

When our feelings are running high, we may need to take a "time-out" in order to deal with them.   Before we can be effective communicators, we must manage our own static. A "time-out" can be anything from sixty seconds to twenty-four hours. A good rule of thumb for raising issues that generate a lot of feeling is to get our own feelings under control first, but not to wait longer than twenty-four hours to deal with the issue. If we wait too long, either we are tempted to ignore the source of the problem or the chasm between the happening that generated the feeling and the discussion of its resolution becomes too wide to bridge. Feelings from others provide static, too. We cannot hear the message under the feelings and the upset person cannot hear any rational input from us until static is addressed. Profanity, crying, ugly gestures, yelling, and overenunciating all obscure the sender's message and block our ability to deal with the issues. Success in dealing with people who are upset is intimately tied to the ability to attend to people's feelings before dealing with specific issues or problems.

In summary, Channel Four is the feeling component in people and it is carried on Channels One, Two, and Three. Feelings are received as static. Meaningful communication cannot take place until feelings are addressed.

Channel Five: Symbolic Communication

The fifth channel of communication is the channel that symbolically carries messages we want to send. Symbolic communication provides a shorthand way for each of us to send a lot of information about ourselves. A wedding band is easy to wear and not nearly as awkward as announcing our marital status in every new situation.

Dress

The style of clothes we wear is one of the principle components of symbolic communication.   At an informal level, we say a lot about ourselves and our roles through the way we dress.   Male executives symbolically communicate their role by coats and ties. We don't expect to find our plumber similarly dressed. Working outfits and uniforms can be functionally symbolic — such as painter pants or a stethoscope around the neck — or they can be symbolic only. A white nurse's uniform is an example of the latter. It helps us to distinguish nurses from patients and is meant to connote the cleanliness of a medical setting.

People tell us a lot about themselves through their personal choice in clothing. A man in a business suit, a man in jeans, a western shirt, and cowboy boots, and a man in fitted Italian casual wear are each sending a different symbolic message.

Utilizing symbolic messages

Symbolic messages are all around us. Cars, jewelry, hairstyles, photographs, credit cards, and home decor say a lot about their owners. The task for communicators is to be sure their symbolic choices send the appropriate message. If we want to be taken seriously as a business person, we wear appropriate business clothes. If we are working with a troubled blue-collar family, we don't use personal examples about housekeepers or children's college experiences. If we are talking to an elderly hard-of-hearing person, we symbolically communicate respect by asking him to let us know if he's having trouble hearing. When we give customers and clients our business card, we are symbolically stating that we are accessible. Wiping our feet before entering someone's home is a symbolic (as well as a practical) gesture.

We also must scan Channel Five carefully to receive the messages of other people. If we call on a friend whose home is filled with pictures of family or bowling trophies and we don't comment on these items, we are missing the message and perhaps "the boat." Channel Five is invaluable in making positive contact and in dealing with upset persons. When we observe that someone has spent time on personal grooming, we can feel more secure if we choose to comment sincerely on their appearance.

A young boy was brought before a juvenile judge for truancy and other delinquent behaviors. His parents, who were seated in the courtroom, were required to cooperate in the treatment process. The judge wishing to make a positive impact on the boy's life, said: "If you don't get a good education, you'll end up nothing more than a common laborer." You could see the father visibly wince as he sat in the courtroom in denim overalls and workingman's boots. By not utilizing information sent on Channel Five, the judge was disregardng important symbolic information and perhaps costing parental cooperation.

In summary, Channel Five, the symbolic communication channel, allows each of us to say a lot about ourselves in shorthand. Channel Five provides us access to the things people consider important.

Channel Six: Territory

The sixth channel of communication is one of territory. The use of physical space and the management of personal physical and psychological territory are the components of Channel Six.

Personal space: Physical

All people have functionally distinct areas of physical space surrounding them.   The core area around each of us (anything less than about 18 inches) is our intimate zone.   There are only two ways a person should ever enter another person's intimate zone.   The first is by invitation.   Invitation means that Channels One, Two, and Three say "come on in."   The only other reason for being in another person's intimate zone is by function.   Two or more people working together on something that requires closeness may need to be less than 18 inches from one another.   When a person inappropriately enters someone's intimate zone, the focus and goal of the invaded person becomes one of removing the intruder from the intimate zone.   No real communication is possible under these circumstances.   By the same token, intimate communication needs to take place in the intimate zone.   Very personal interactions can be upsetting and sometimes even impossible when executed beyond the intimate personal zone.

From 18 inches to 36 inches is the territory within which "business" is conducted.   It is about the distance of a handshake. Beyond 36 inches is stranger territory. It is very difficult to have any interpersonal communication in stranger territory. People have been known to escalate into upset persons when "business" interactions have been attempted across too wide an area. The physician's receptionist who shares test results across the waiting room or the bank teller who announces an overdrawn account to a customer several yards away is violating good communication practices. So, too, is the parent who continually reprimands publicly or the spouse who belittles the partner outside the appropriate territorial boundary.

Personal space: Psychological

In addition to our personal physical zones, each of us has psychological zones that have similar characteristics to our physical zones. Our core psychological space is made up of things that significantly define who we are. The person who puts much of his or her energy into a career or the person who is a very invested parent has these roles imbedded in his or her core psychological area. The next ring in our personal psychological space includes those roles and definitions about ourselves that we consider a part of us but are not crucial. For example, some men and women would designate parenthood in the core psychological territory while placing community activities in the secondary area. For other people being good citizens is also very much a part of their sense of identification. For these people, community activities would join parenthood in the core area. Beyond our symbolic 36 inch psychological territory are those things that are not a part of our identity at all — the "not-me" qualities. Just as a person may feel attacked if his or her core psychological territory is invaded, so he or she might feel attacked if the "not-me" qualities are attributed to him/her.

> A friend of ours is an artist who has also become extremely successful both through the recognition of her work but also because of her excellent skills at marketing. Because she thinks of herself as an artist and not as a businesswoman, she dismisses the skillful marketer part as just luck. She chooses to have the role of businesswoman in the "not-me" psychological space. She would take offense at being referred to as a good businesswoman.

Territory and Upset Persons

Psychological and physical territory are critical when we are dealing with upset persons. Old western movies abound with examples of escalating bar-room brawls based on invasion of physical and psychological territory — the "that's my barstool" or "that's my girl" mentality. In making positive contact, we need to recognize the other person's territory and be careful not to invade it. If we have already overstepped our bounds, we have to get out of the territory as quickly and carefully as possible. Upset is frequently the response to territorial invasion.

Nonpersonal physical territory

The arrangment and utilization of the physical space around us has implications for communication. We can become irritated if there are insufficient cues telling us where to go in order to accomplish our purpose efficiently. Furniture can be either a communication barrier or a useful and comfortable part of our space. The appropriate use of physical territory involves arranging it to maximize function and to minimize emotional backlash. In order to accomplish this satisfactorily, it is necessary to be clear on goals. How close do you want others, physically and psychologically? What will maximize the efficient flow of work? What do you want your space to say to others? These are questions that need answering.

A couple in marital counseling shared that most of their sexual contact ended in upset because each of them feared being interrupted by the appearance of one of their children in the bedroom. It wasn't always the actual invasion by a child that divided their attention but the possibility of such an interruption. Significant upset was reduced when the counselor suggested a lock for the bedroom door. The parents needed reassurance that private parental space was not a statement about their accessibility to their children.

Territorial Rules

Here are some territorial rules to keep in mind:

1)   Space is divided more or less equally among the number of individuals who share it. (Observe people on elevators.)

2)   The less physical space available to us, the more we utilize psychological barriers to provide privacy. (Think about differences in people's behavior with strangers on the street in crowded urban areas and on the street of a small rural community.)

3)   Physical territory often serves a symbolic purpose. (Observe the offices of executives, as opposed to the work areas of entry-level employees.)

4)   A person can compensate for some territorial problems by how they position themselves. (Observe

how people stay behind barriers when they want distance and come out from behind them when they don't.)

5) For maximum communication, advance to the edge of your territory and invite other people to come to the edge of theirs. Escort people into your space in order to be able to escort them out. (Observe your feelings when the person with whom you have an appointment greets you, and takes you into the office versus being told, "Go to the third office on the left." Observe the host or hostess who greets you at the door versus the person who yells "come in" without turning off the TV.)

In summary, Channel Six, territory, is an important communication channel, especially as it relates to upset persons. Personal territory and physical territory can be managed so as to maximize their efficacy in interpersonal relations.

Channel Seven: Behavior

The seventh and final channel of communication is our behavior — our intentional (and sometimes not so intentional) actions. While what we say and how we say it *is* important, what we do becomes the bottom line determinant of successful relationships.

It is important to do what we say we will do. For example, if we tell someone we care about them and like being with them, those words are meaningless unless we arrange to spend time together. Similarly, if we say our faith is important to us while neither involving ourselves in religious activities nor leading our lives based on the tenets of our faith, we are not behaving consistently with what we say is significant to us.

We never make promises we can't keep nor threats we don't have the power or inclination to execute. Rather than threaten, we inform. We inform our children of the potential consequences of rule breaking. We inform others about what they can and cannot expect us to do. If we can't keep a promise, we inform the person to whom we made the promise that we are no longer able to carry it out. For the most successful interactions, use follow-through and follow-up. In summary, Channel Seven says that what we do is the bottom line of the communication process.

THE SEVEN CHANNELS

The seven channels of communication described above are the basic building blocks of communication.

All interactions include these seven channels in both sending and receiving. Good communicators successfully communicate the same message on all seven channels while scanning the channels of other people to be sure they are receiving the intended message.

Channels Three (body language), Four (feelings), and Five (symbolic communication) come into focus first. We look to see who the approaching persons are, the ways in which they present themselves, and what feelings they engender in us. At an almost subconscious level we determine spatial issues. Eventually we decipher their message by scanning Channels One (language), Two (manner), and Three (body language).

Messages have three components: the affective or feeling component; the cognitive or content component; and the behavioral or action-oriented component.

You can see that communication is a complex process. But like driving a car, we have been at it so long that we put the components together without much thought. As you focus on handling upset people, we ask you purposefully to be more aware of your own and other people's channels.

CHAPTER THREE
CONCEPTUAL FRAMEWORKS FOR
DEALING WITH UPSET PERSONS

In the middle of a seemingly pleasant family dinner, Jack described a remodeling project he had in mind for turning the basement into a small usable study. Jack's grown son began making suggestions about how Jack should carry out the project. First he told Jack he should consider putting the study where the garage was rather than in the basement in order to have a room with windows. Then Jack's son and his wife both said that they didn't think walnut paneling would be attractive. Within five minutes Jack's temper erupted and after shouting that he would fix his house "any darn way I want," he left the table and slammed out of the house to take a walk and cool down. When he returned, his son, daughter-in-law, and wife all told him he was "acting like a baby." Jack ended up quietly angry and sullen the rest of the evening. No one left the dinner feeling good.

Upset interactions often seem to be wild, unmanageable happenings. When we are a part of them, we can feel totally helpless and out of control. Yet there *is* order in the chaos. We don't have to be as helpless as we feel. Understanding the process of what is happening to the other person as well as what is happening to us is vital if we are going to be more in

44

control of ourselves and help others to control themselves. What we need in order to understand this process is a framework or theoretical model within which interactions can be systematized. This chapter will describe two such frameworks. The first, Transactional Analysis, is helpful in understanding upset interactions. Rational-Emotive Therapy, one of the more cognitive therapies, is helpful in the self-management of behavior. Both will be employed throughout the remainder of the book as we focus on the specifics of dealing with upset persons.

TRANSACTIONAL ANALYSIS: A MODEL FOR UNDERSTANDING INTERACTIONS

Transactional analysis (T.A.) is a method for dissecting an interpersonal transaction. Eric Berne, the originator of T.A., defined a transaction as a unit of social intercourse. Sharing a common T.A. terminology helps us to conceptualize and systematize our interactions. Standardizing the language assists us not only in looking at what happens in our interactions with upset people, but also assists us in changing our behavior in order to prevent or diminish upsets.

Think, for a moment, about a person in your life

you know very well. You can usually visualize this person in a number of different ways. He or she might be laughing at something funny, looking depressed, or feeling angry. You might picture this person talking to and petting a dog. Perhaps the person is scolding a child for talking back. Finally, you might imagine this person at a business meeting conducting himself or herself with propriety while making a staff presentation and fielding questions. It might be difficult to remember that this reasonable, effective businessperson was having a temper tantrum over a scraped fender just the night before. Each of us has many dimensions. According to T.A., the various aspects of our personalities can be classified into three states: the child state, the parent state, and the adult state.

The Child Ego State

Our child ego state is the one with which we enter the world. The child part of us focuses on getting our needs met. The child in each of us is small, clumsy, dependent, and without words. Since this little person lacks words, reactions are all in the form of feelings. It is the body of feelings related to being dependent and trying to get our needs met that we carry through life with us in the form of our child ego state. We can be transferred into our child state any time we are involved in transactions that recreate situations from our childhood and that engender in us the same feelings we felt then. Our child has the capacity to be angry, rebellious, frightened, happy, loving, sad, and so forth. The goals of the child are to be liked, to be admired, to have fun, and to have needs met.

The manipulative child

Sometimes in the process of having our needs met as children, we learned some manipulative behaviors that we then try to utilize to get our needs met later in life.

> As a small child, Phillip's mother would frequently break down and let Phillip have his way after he carried on and screamed so long that she felt she could stand no more. As an adult, Phillip escalates his abrasive anger higher and higher when he is crossed. In most cases, Phillip can hold out longer than his adversary and he ends up getting his way.

The part of our child ego state that uses manipulation to get needs met is called the "manipulative child." We must be careful not to reward upset people who are escalating unacceptable behaviors and operating out of their manipulative child state. If we are going to meet their requests, we need to do so before they feel the need to raise the ante. If we are not going to meet their requests, we must not allow ourselves to be intimidated into changing our minds.

Upset people are almost always in their child ego state. This ego state (their feelings) must be addressed before any problems can be handled. We'll have more to say about this in Chapter Five.

The Parent Ego State

Our parent ego state is the repository for the recording of events as we perceived them in the early years of our lives. These recordings or parent tapes come from the examples and pronouncements of our parents or other significant people in our lives. The messages on the tapes were recorded without editing. They include all the prohibitions, admonitions and rules both stated and set by example. We stored them without question. The goal of the parent ego state is to be superior and helpful.

The critical parent

The parent ego state has two parts: the critical parent and the caring parent. Each of the parent states has a different impact upon people who are upset. When a child falls and skins his or her knee, the parent may say to the child, "You shouldn't have been running so fast. If you'd been more careful, you wouldn't have hurt yourself." Such an admonition is typical of the critical parent.

All of the rules that govern us as children are parentally inspired. It's a safe bet to suggest that all of the imperatives — you should, you must, you ought to, why can't you, don't you see, etc. — are pronounced by the critical parent embedded within each of us. Sometimes we don't even know why we carry these rules around and insist they should be applied in our present lives.

I (Pennie) remember my mother teaching me how to make chicken soup — a skill no nurturing mother (we'll discuss nurturing in the next section) worth her salt is without. One of the unbreakable rules of chicken soup-making was that the soup had to be skimmed just after it came to a boil. For years, I followed this maternal "must." One day I raised the inevitable question. "Mom," I said, "why is it we always skim the soup after it comes to a boil?" Her answer was the classic demonstration of how parent tapes are transferred from one generation to another — this parent tape being one she learned by example rather than by verbal rule. She said, "When I was a child my grandmother, who was very poor, always skimmed the soup. Since she never threw away anything edible, I just assumed the skimmed part of the soup must be inedible." So much for that "should." I either had to learn a more significant reason to skim chicken soup or not shake my finger at myself in a critical parent way if I chose to avoid this step.

The caring parent

Now that we've observed what our critical parent says when a child skins his or her knee, let's look at the caring parent. The caring parent comes out of a very different place and says to that same child, "Oh, you skinned your knee. I'll bet it hurts. Come here and let me kiss it and make it better."

Each of us carries both a critical parent and a caring parent within us. The problem in dealing with upset persons is that often the natural inclination is to respond out of the critical parent when in fact we would do much better to respond out of the caring parent. The friend who is disappointed by your inability to share a last minute dinner invitation will react better to a simple "I'm sorry we are unable to enjoy dinner together" than to "If you had called me earlier in the week, then we'd have been able to arrange dinner together." The way in which the feelings of the child state (of upset people) get handled most satisfactorily is by responding as a caring parent. The formula for handling upset people in Chapter Five will say more about this.

The Adult Ego State

The third ego state is the adult ego state. The adult is the rational part of us. It operates on data gathering and data processing. It begins developing when we are very young. Our life experiences give us data and information that challenge both the taught concepts of the parent and the feelings of the child. The adult part of us figures things out by looking at facts. It is unemotional. "Adult," by the way, is not synonymous with "mature." The goal of the adult is to be competent.

A common mistake in dealing with an upset person is to move into the adult state too soon. As was suggested earlier, upset people are in the child ego state and need a caring parent. Only when we have appropriately dealt with the child's feelings can we successfully move into the adult ego state and turn our attention to solving the problem presented.

Each of us is made up of all three parts. All of the ego states are equally important. None is superior. However, we need to have enough adult operating to assess the situation and to help the parent and the child make decisions and solve problems.

Transactional Analysis and Upset People

In the scenario that opened this chapter, Jack's family may have thought they were behaving as logical, rational adults, but they were talking as critical parents. Characteristically, Jack responded as an upset, angry child. If he was hoping for either approval or adult suggestions, he was disappointed. He was left feeling inadequate and defensive. Anyone at this dinner could have positively affected the outcome of the senario if they had understood what was happening and managed their behavior accordingly. T.A. provides a useful model for understanding ourselves and other people. It can help us to quickly defuse a potentially difficult situation — first by responding from the caring parent state and then by moving to the adult state. It is not easy to manage ourselves in such a way that we stay in charge of ourselves, set an appropriate tone for interactions, and remain open and nondefensive. What is a key for managing our own behavior? Let's turn our attention to one of the cognitive therapies, Albert Ellis' Rational-Emotive Therapy.

RATIONAL-EMOTIVE THERAPY: A MODEL OF BEHAVIORAL SELF-MANAGEMENT

Our behavior is affected by a number of things including expectations, perceptions, the meaning we attach to things, our value systems, past experiences, and the way in which we talk to ourselves. Rather than always using the adult to motivate behavior, people sometimes act out of the child or the parent ego state. In formulating his theory of Rational-Emotive Therapy (R.E.T.), Ellis describes these nonadult behavioral antecedents as irrational thinking or as being the result of a faulty inner dialogue. Irrational thinking is responsible for a great deal of human discomfort. In a variety of contexts and relationships, our anxieties could be reduced significantly if we did not talk to ourselves irrationally.

The ABC's

Ellis teaches what he calls the ABC's of behavior. An Activating Event (A) seems to cause an emotional reaction or Consequence (C) in people. However, A does not really cause C. On closer inspection, it becomes clear that C was more likely caused by the Belief System (B) or how people talk to themselves.

Schematically, then, we have:

> (A)ctivating Experience
>
> Rational (B)elief
>
> Appropriate (C)onsequences

or:

> (A)ctivating Experience
>
> Irrational (B)elief
>
> Inappropriate (C)onsequence

Let's look at an example of how this might work. The spouse of a close friend from work suddenly dies. You want to make a condolence call on your friend. Your inner dialogue might be:

> This is a painful time for Mary. I'd like to go see her to express my sadness for her, my caring, and to let her know I'll be around if she needs something. If I put myself in her shoes, I'd appreciate the visit and expressions of sympathy. I don't need to *do* anything. I just need to go and be there.

With an inner dialogue like the one above, you are likely to go to see Mary with little anxiety because you haven't laid enormous expectations on yourself. All you have to do is pay a visit and be there for her. This most likely meets Mary's needs and your needs. How might the same scenario play out if you substitute irrational beliefs or faulty self-talk at step B? In that case your inner dialogue might be:

> I want to go to see Mary, but I'm not sure she wants me to do that. What will I say to her? It's always so hard to think of the right things to say to someone who is grieving. What if she cries? What if I cry? What if she thinks I have ulterior motives? Maybe she'll think I didn't know her husband well enough to pay a condolence visit. Maybe there will be so many people there she won't notice that I came and I'll feel left out.

With this kind of inner dialogue you are placing tremendous expectations on yourself and Mary. The result or consequence of such self-talk is likely to be one that will not mutually meet your needs or Mary's needs. You are likely to decide not to pay the call or, if you do make the visit, you may be self-conscious and unspontaneous. Worse yet, you may place inappropriate expectations on a grieving friend and become disappointed in how she responds to your visit. Your expectations are unlikely to be met. Mary may lose the comfort of a caring friend.

It is clear from the above example that self-talk rather than the activating event, in this case the need to call on a bereaved friend, is responsible for the behavioral outcome.

Four Irrational Beliefs

Ellis describes four kinds of human irrationalities that lead to self-defeating behaviors. Irrational beliefs can be MUSTurbatory — that is, they emanate from an erroneous belief that certain things *must* happen so that we can get our way. "I must do well." "I must be approved of." "I must get what I want." Irrational thinking can also spring from "awfulizing," "can't stand its," and "damning of yourself and others."   The inner dialogues of these three irrationalities go something like this:

> "It was awful that I forgot Jason Keller's name. He must think I'm stupid. He'll probably never do business with me again."

> "If everything doesn't run perfectly for the annual fundraiser, I won't be able to stand the humiliation. I just don't know what I'll do. I won't be able to stand it."

> "I hate myself for making that stupid mistake. How could I be so dumb? I never do anything right."

D and E

Improved interactions necessitate that we move from responding out of a child or parent state into using our adult state. Ellis suggests that if faulty inner dialogues and irrational beliefs get in the way of effective functioning, it is necessary to Dispute (D) those irrational ideas in your head in order to produce a new and more desirable consequence or Effect (E). Reactions to upset customers are a case in point. Imagine a sarcastic, upset customer approaching a service representative at a local utility company.

> "I don't know why I had to wait ten minutes to get through to *you*. You'd think with the outrageous rates consumers pay for electricity, this company could hire enough employees."

How does the service representative talk to him/herself? An irrational belief would be that the representative is being picked on unfairly or is somehow responsible for the customer's upset because energy costs are high. Placating or defensive behavior might result. A more rational inner dialogue would be:

> "This man is upset about his high electric bill. He is not angry with me. I do not have to solve all his financial problems. Nor do I have to defend myself or my company. I do have to acknowledge, understand, and respond to his feelings. If I can help him to solve his problem, I will do my best."

Rational Self-Talk and Upset Persons

Dealing with upset persons requires that we *not* operate out of the child or critical parent ego state. Therefore, some kind of internal mechanism is needed to help control natural, instinctive, but unproductive behaviors. R.E.T. says that often behavior is motivated by what people say to themselves. This suggests that anger, as well as other feelings, is a choice. If anger is a choice, we can choose to respond to upset people in a variety of other ways. We have the choice of getting angry, becoming hostile, or yelling. We can also choose alternative behaviors by talking to ourselves in such a way as to control the level of our upset. When we talk to ourselves rationally, we are more successful in our dealings with upset people.

In summary, this chapter has described Transactional Analysis and Rational-Emotive Therapy. T.A. helps us to understand the interactions we have with others. R.E.T. is a useful tool in helping us to control our own feelings and behaviors. Both theories will be used throughout the remainder of the book.

CHAPTER FOUR
MAKING POSITIVE CONTACT

Peter and Marilyn Gold were a gracious host and hostess. They had a knack for putting together interesting groups of people and for giving successful parties. An evening at the Gold's always began with Pete and Marilyn greeting their guests at the door, introducing them to other guests previously unknown to them, and showing them to the food and drinks. Pete and Marilyn knew that the success of the evening often depended on how the evening began.

An ounce of prevention is worth a pound of cure. Similarly, a positive initial interaction diminishes the likelihood of having to contend with an upset person. Making positive contact with people is the obvious first step in any interaction. Before discussing the specific elements of positive contact, let's take a look at two components of the interpersonal process that affect our ability to connect positively with others and to interact successfully with them.

LIKING PEOPLE

Most people have significant social needs. By this we mean that people like to be liked. These social needs are based on the fact that people are dependent upon one another for survival. During infancy, of course, basic survival needs must be met by other people. Throughout our lives, each of us requires a variety of people to meet some of our physical, emotional, social, and sexual needs. This interdependency programs us to like people. Generally, if we don't like people, it is because something in our life is or has been problematic. One element involved in our capacity to like people is self-esteem. If we don't like ourselves, we have trouble liking other people. Virginia Satir, a well-known family therapist, describes each of us as having a pot of self-esteem that we can hoard or share with others. The more full our pot, the more we have to share. If our pot is almost empty, we have very little to give away. People with empty pots don't feel good about themselves and don't feel good about other people. Having few good feelings in reserve impedes our capacity to connect substantively with people. We have more trouble liking other people and they have more trouble liking us.

There is a paradox in this metaphor. Giving good feelings to others brings good feelings back to us. We can replenish our own pots by filling other people's pots. Reaching out and making positive contact helps us like others and therefore ourselves better.   The couple in our opening illustration will no doubt have the opportunity to be future guests at other social gatherings.   Being positive and outgoing hosts will indirectly impact their self-esteem.

A second element that affects our sociability originates in how we have been treated by significant people in our lives. If we have been treated badly, we not only have learned not to trust others, but we also have not had positive contact demonstrated for us. An implicit lack of trust and know-how impedes our willingness and ability to approach others. A paradox exists here, too. Holding back causes others to hold back. Aloofness begets aloofness. This then reinforces our belief that others are cold and distant and not to be trusted.   Reaching out and making positive contact is more reinforcing because it produces positive behavior in others.

A third factor affecting our liking of people involves how we remember our past interactions with people. If we remember only negative interactions, we tend to view people negatively.   The natural tendency is to remember the one or two negative interactions of the day rather than the eight or ten positive ones. This kind of selective recall has an impact on how we feel about people. A more balanced view of interactions with people engenders more positive feelings about them.

Finally, how we feel about others is affected by how we feel about what we do. It is important to like what we do — jobs, family life, recreation and hobbies. Time is the one resource that is distributed equally to everyone. The task is to be sure to do the best possible job of spending it.

Liking what we do correlates positively with how we do it. If our job does not satisfactorily address our interests and aptitudes or our personality, we may need to rethink career goals. If we recognize that much of our nonworking time is spent unsatisfactorily, it may be time to explore alternative lifestyle possibilities.

It is not selfish to work toward liking what we do. How we feel about how we spend our life affects everyone our life touches. Obviously, no one is content with every aspect of life all the time. The goal is to make what we do count for us.

LETTING PEOPLE KNOW WE LIKE THEM

Liking people is only the first step in making positive contact. The second step is letting others know we like them. Each of us varies in our ability to reach out and become involved with people. The individual capacity to do this lies on a continuum. People on one end of the continuum find it very easy to show people they like them. People at the other end find it very difficult.

<--->

Very easy   Very difficult
to show people   to show people
you like them   you like them

People on the "easy" end of the continuum probably already know a lot about setting the tone and being in charge of interactions. They are also probably aware that their positive approach to other folks is reciprocated. This, in turn, enhances self-confidence and self-esteem, making it even easier to continue to show liking for others. All in all, it is a very circular process.

Of course, the circular process may be a negative one for those folks who find it difficult to show other people that they like them. This negative circularity reinforces the difficulty of reaching out to other people.

If you fall on the "difficult" end of the continuum, it probably means that you are either shy and fearful of rejection or that you have not cultivated your interpersonal skills to their fullest. In short, you're either scared or you don't know how. In either case, the only remedy is practice, practice, and more practice.

Before reading on, please take time to assess yourself on the following shyness inventory. There is no score on this inventory. Rather, it is designed to have you stop and take stock of yourself in regard to shyness. You might also find it helpful to use this inventory as a feedback tool. Ask a loved one, a friend, or a coworker to share their perceptions of you by answering the questions on the inventory as they pertain to you. It can be helpful to learn how others perceive us.

SELF-ASSESSMENT OF SHYNESS

1) Is shyness ever a problem for you?

2) Have any of the following sometimes made you feel shy?

Fear of rejection	Fear of evaluation
Lack of confidence	Fear of intimacy
Lack of social skills	Personal inadequacies

3) Do other people see you as shy? Are you able to conceal your shyness?

4) Do other people see you as unfriendly or aloof?

5) Are there specific situations in which you feel shy? For example, in large groups, where you don't know anyone, where you are the center of attention, in social situations, etc. List these.

6) Are you more shy around certain kinds of people? For example, around authorities, strangers, people of the opposite sex, relatives, people of different backgrounds, etc. List these.

7) Do you experience physical reactions to shyness such as blushing, perspiring, heart-pounding, etc.? List these.

8) Do you think you are self-conscious?

9) Do you have difficulty making eye contact with people? Smiling at others? Introducing yourself?

10) Do you struggle talking to others—speaking too quietly, not thinking of anything to say, being silent, stuttering, rambling, etc.? List these.

11) Are you aware of any personal consequences of your shyness? Costs? Benefits? List these.

THE TACTFUL ACRONYM

If you like people and want them to know you like them, you already are well motivated for making positive contact. A useful frame of reference for making positive connections with people is an acronym that helps people remember seven key elements that comprise the process of reaching out to people. The acronym T-A-C-T-F-U-L is also a reminder that positive contact involves approaching others in a way that enhances the likelihood of a successful interaction. Positive contact requires tact.

T=Territory

The "T" in TACTFUL stands for *territory*. Territory has been discussed in some detail in Chapter Two. The important positive contact premise about territory is to come to the edge of our territory and encourage other people to come to the edge of their's. Moving to the edge of our territory is accomplished physically by such things as taking community activities to the group who can best use the services, by coming out from behind a desk, by going to the door of an adolescent's room, or by going to the home of a friend who is bereaved. Symbolically, we demonstrate being at the edge of our territory by doing as much as possible to be helpful without intruding: "May I hold your umbrella while you find what you need in your purse?" "Before we get any further, let me tell you what this volunteer job entails." An offer of Kleenex to a person who is crying, or making eye contact to indicate that we'll be with someone who is waiting symbolically exemplifies coming to the edge of our territory and inviting others to do likewise.

However, it is also important to communicate a respect for limits. We offer a chair without forcing a person to sit down. We indicate a willingness to listen without demanding a person talk. We knock at the door of an adolescent's room or a colleague's office, but we do not enter without an invitation. The guideline is to come to the edge of our territory, not to barge into someone else's territory.

A=Appropriate Facial Expression

In our intitial contact with people, it is important to greet them with an appropriate facial expression. In the absence of cues that would indicate otherwise, smiling is the most appropriate way to reach out nonverbally to others. A *smile* is a universal human connector. It is almost impossible to be unresponsive to a person who greets you with a smile. If you doubt this, try smiling to salespeople, people you pass in your office building, or shoppers at the grocery store. Practice smiling over the telephone. A smile can be heard over the telephone because our voices resonate higher when we are smiling. When we smile we are likely to bring out the positive in other people.

> When my (Don's) Grandmother Bertie first entered the nursing home where she lived the last twelve years of her life, she got the nickname "the you can give me something special lady." She'd approach various residents saying, "You know you can give me something special." "What can we give you when we have nothing to give?" they'd respond. Bertie would say, "You can give me a smile." In her quiet way, Bertie brought much joy to her Texas nursing home.

A smile is an appropriate facial expression in most, but not all, situations. Obviously we don't smile at angry, upset or grieving people.

C=Contact

The phrase positive contact underscores the need for *contact* with people. In order for a conversation to be successful, people need to experience the feeling of connectedness, to feel as if an invisible thread exists connecting them with the other person. There are several ways that such contact can be demonstrated in any interaction: through *eye contact* ; through *short verbal phrases* that indicate we have heard what the other person is saying; and through *non-verbal behaviors* such as head nods or other gestures that demonstrate we are following the gist of what the other person is saying.

The impact of *eye contact* is immediate in making positive contact. Eye contact indicates involvement. When people use eye contact it is as if they are saying, "I'm home" or "You've gotten my attention." Eye contact provides a symbolic connection.

Not everyone is comfortable with eye contact. Some people have difficulty using it. Early training has a lot to do with individual differences. For instance, some children are told, "Always look at me when I'm talking to you." Others are instructed that respect and deference are shown to one's elders by averting the eyes. Eye contact is not synonymous with staring. It involves a combination of both looking at the other person and also looking away. Observe your comfort level with eye contact. Notice how others respond to various degrees of eye contact. If you are not comfortable with eye contact, practice using it. Practice will help put you more at ease.

We need to show people we are attuned to what they are saying. Head *nods* signal that we are following the gist of a conversation. Being listened to and understood are important to people. Therefore we use the nods as one way to let them know we hear what they are saying and understand their feelings.

Head nods, of course, cannot be seen over the telephone, so in their place we substitute appropriate grunts and verbal expressions. These include "uh huh," "check," "yup," "gotcha," and "I'm following," which can be included in face-to-face contact as well. The important thing is to let the other person know you are still tuned in. As a sender, be sure you are getting the appropriate signals from your listeners. If not, it is wise to check in with them to be certain that they are listening and understand what they hear.

T=Thorough

Thoroughness is a theme of *The Upset Book*. One cause of upset in other people is their belief that they have been short-shrifted in some way. An easy way to prevent upset in other people is to be meticulously thorough in our dealings with them. If we are thorough, there is less opportunity for something to go wrong. The added bonus in thoroughness is the response of other people. Once they see that we are attending to them with care and in detail, they are less likely to respond with anger or upset.

F = Forward

Chapter One described the natural tendency to want to run the other way when someone is approaching angrily or upset. Similarly, if we have made a mistake, our inclination is to want to keep it a secret. The "F" for *forward* signifies that making positive contact requires us to come foward, particularly at those times when a backdoor exit would feel like the perfect escape. For example, an angry congregant prefers the minister who moves quickly forward and says, "You seem upset about something. Can I be of help?" The congregant is likely to relax because it appears that someone actually wants to assist in the resolution of the problem. The minister who comes forward is in direct contrast to the one who, because of discomfort in dealing with upset, ignores the congregant's upset. The congregant then ends up with initial (primary) upset and added dismay at being ignored (secondary upset).

> When I (Pennie) was a child, curiosity compelled me to completely disassemble my mother's watch, which had been a tenth

anniversary gift from my father. I may have been adept at taking the watch apart but I was totally incapable of reversing the process. In dismay and fear I disposed of the evidence. In so doing, I quickly learned that I had more than doubled my trouble. I was confronted with a mother who was not only upset because I had taken her watch apart but who was absolutely beside herself because I had thrown it away. Both she and I wished that I had come forward after the first indiscretion and confessed my crime.

Similarly:

We have wondered for years about the "chicken or egg" effect at seminars we teach. Those who sit toward the front of the room seem to enjoy the seminar more and get more from it than those who fill up the most distant seats. Do those who sit toward the front already have a more positive attitude or does coming forward help to make experiences more meaningful?

We believe that moving forward pays dividends in our personal lives, professional lives, and in commercial situations. Coming forward when we have made mistakes or are faced with an unpleasant situation has fewer repercussions than avoidance or escape. Coming forward to partake of life's experiences adds richness to our world.

U=Understand

All people appreciate being understood and are much less likely to become upset if they feel they are approached with understanding. When we understand another person, we are making positive contact with him or her. Understanding other people is valuable in preventing upset and equally valuable in managing situations where people are already upset. In order to understand other people, it is necessary to be open to what they have to say. We need both to be *willing* to communicate openly with others and also to *show* our openness. There is no room for a critical, evaluative mind-set in dealing with people.

L=Listen

Listening sounds like an easy behavior, yet it is one of the most difficult. We have all had the experience of talking to someone who is pretending to listen. We rarely are fooled! We know the difference between really being heard and a fake listening response. Good listening has prevented much potential upset. Not listening, on the other hand, often has been the harbinger of upset to come.

Skill-Building Activities For T-A-C-T-F-U-L

A few activities are listed in this section to help you develop the ability to make positive contact. As has been indicated, approaching people and responding to them is an acquired skill. Our everyday interactions with people are the most effective activity for developing positive contact skills. The following activities can be practiced in your daily life.

1) At business and social gatherings practice approaching people you don't know with the idea of learning about them. Avoid talking only to those people you already know. Use TACTFUL.

2) Take opportunities to introduce yourself to people you don't know. Smile, extend your hand, identify yourself and say, "I don't believe we've met before."

3) If you think someone is upset, check this out with him or her at the earliest opportunity. "You seem upset. Is something bothering you?" Come forward rather than avoid a potential issue.

4) Ask coworkers, family, or friends for feedback about your style. Do they feel you are involved when you interact? Do they think you are open to what they are saying? Do your nonverbal gestures indicate you are following what they are saying? You can make copies

of the shyness inventory and the personal communication inventory and ask family members, coworkers, or friends to fill them out about you.

5) Practice observing people. Look for qualities you like and admire. Do not focus on flaws. Then practice sharing something positive with them. Keep written lists of qualities you like in other people. Practice writing a note or memo of appreciation.

In addition to the TACTFUL elements, there are at least three other elements involved in making positive contact. Discussion of these follows.

REMEMBERING NAMES

A person's name is his or her own unique, personal label. Learning, remembering, and being able to use a person's name is very important in making positive contact.

We can learn a person's name in several ways. They can tell us. We can ask. We can learn it by observing it on a credit card, their records, or other paper work. We can learn it by being told by someone else. Those of us who want to make a good positive connection with someone will be certain to take the time and trouble to learn the name.

Mr. L. frequently bumped into us at community functions. Since he never seemed to remember our names, we always reintroduced ourselves. In a moment of extreme honesty, Mr. L. said, "I'm terrible at names but to tell you the truth, I never remember names 'cause I never really hear them in the first place."

Like Mr. L., some of you may be saying, "I can never remember peoples' names." And like Mr. L., the most common reason for being unable to remember a name is that we haven't really heard it and learned it in the first place. So, the first key to remembering a name is to listen to it carefully. Then use it. Repeat it. If it's a difficult or foreign name, continue trying to pronounce it correctly until you and the person whose name you are learning are satisfied. If you can immediately use a name three times after learning it, you will be more successful at remembering it. When you meet many people at one time, there is less expectation that you will remember everyone's name. But follow the above suggestions and you will be surprised at how many names you can learn at a time.

Once you have the name in your repertoire, by all means use it. As you talk to people, punctuate your conversation with their names. It personalizes the interactions. People feel unique and special. Later, when we talk about the specifics of dealing with very angry or upset people, we will again talk about the importance of names. Staying angry is more difficult when you are not anonymous.

One of the frequently asked questions about names is when to use first and last names. The setting, the age of the parties involved, and the nature of the interaction all play a role in such a decision. A good rule of thumb, however, is that when in doubt, it is safer to be more formal. It is much easier for a person to request, "Call me Tom," than it is for him to say, "I prefer to be called Mr. Smith."

A corollary question about names is, "When is it appropriate to use Mrs., Ms., or Miss?" Fortunately, this question is becoming increasingly easier to answer as the use of Ms. becomes more and more acceptable. Good judgment is invaluable. If, for example, you are interacting with a 78-year-old woman wearing a wedding band, you are reasonably safe using Mrs. With most young women, Ms. is the appropriate choice.

A closing point of information. Anytime you forget someone's name don't be afraid to ask again. Asking says you care enough to seek it.

FREE INFORMATION

The more quickly you learn about another person, the more able you are to tailor your interactions specifically to them. The quicker you gain information about another, the more readily a positive contact can be cemented. Free information is information people share about themselves without being asked. They do this in several ways. Sometimes they simply tell us. In the course of talking, others share bits and pieces of information about themselves and their lives.

> Margaret needed help in her business but had only enough money for a half-time position. At a community meeting, she met Ted who mentioned that he would be taking early retirement the following month. He also mentioned his work history which included experience that might be applicable to the position Margaret needed to fill. The next day Margaret contacted Ted. A part-time position was very appealing to him. It would allow him to make a transition into retirement. The free information was probably responsible for Ted being offered the job and for the solution to Margaret's dilemma.

Sometimes free information is available on Channel Five (symbolic communication). If people have pictures of children and grandchildren in their office or home, it is a statement of what's important to them. A person who dresses fashionably is sending a message different from the person who dresses casually or conservatively. Homes or offices that are neat as pins, or are filled with art, house plants, or sports memorabilia each give us a lot of free information about the person who lives or works there. Even a person's car is a symbolic statement about him or her.   Good powers of observation are invaluable tools. Utilizing free information as we deal with others helps us personalize our interactions.

PERSONALIZING

Using names and free information is part of a larger process called personalizing. Positive contact involves personalizing.   Personalizing is custom tailoring to other people what we say and do. It lets folks know that we are aware of their individuality.   It includes all the little touches that help the other person know we see them as important, as unique, and as worthy of our time and effort.

Skill-Building Activities For Remembering Names, Free Information and Personalizing

1)   When you meet someone new, listen carefully to their name. If necessary, ask them to repeat it, help you

pronounce it, or spell it. Use their name at least three times, even if the interaction is brief. Do this whenever you are meeting someone new.

2)   When you are with people, be aware of things they tell you about themselves, other people, or their situation that you did not ask about. Are there parts of the free information you are filing away? Can you think of ways to use the information that might be helpful to you and the other person?

3)   Select one or two people on whom to practice personalizing skills. Keep the focus on the other person. Ask questions and share information that uniquely addresses the person's interests. Use their name frequently in the conversation. Observe their channels of communication in order to get a reading of how they are experiencing the interaction.

We have described the art of making positive contact — the style of interacting that we hope prevents people from escalating their upset. An ounce of prevention may be worth a pound of cure, but the already sick person requires treatment. Positive contact is useful in establishing relationships, in maintaining good relationships, and in preventing secondary upset. But, what about interacting with the person who is already upset, angry, depressed, or grieving? We need more than positive contact skills for such delicate situations.

CHAPTER FIVE
DEALING WITH UPSET PEOPLE

Ben's mother knew that whenever Ben asked for hot chocolate, it meant he was upset about something. She'd carefully prepare the hot chocolate after which the two of them would sit down together, sipping the cocoa and talking. What usually happened was that Ben talked about what was bothering him while his mother listened attentively. Sometimes Ben's problem got solved. Sometimes it didn't. Often Ben forgot to drink his hot chocolate. But he always felt better afterward.

Those of us who have had the good fortune to be listened to attentively at a time of upset understand the relief Ben experienced from the warmth of his mother's listening. Those of us who have had our feelings ignored, mocked, or dismissed understand the frustration of unsoothed upset. The principles which Ben's mother used in responding to his upset can be applied to dealing with upset people in general.

Most of us will find ourselves face-to-face with upset people from time to time. The occassional need to deal with upset people exists even when we have used all the principles of positive contact. The following formula provides the basic recipe for dealing with people who are upset.

THE FORMULA FOR DEALING WITH UPSET PEOPLE

There are five ingredients in the formula for dealing with upset people. These are: listening, empathizing, clarifying, problem solving, and closing. After we describe and discuss each ingredient, we will provide some practice excercises that are designed to help you increase your skills in dealing with upset people.

Listening

Good listening is easier said than done. It takes skill and practice. It requires giving total attention to the other person. Listening involves carefully scanning the other person's seven channels. When we practice listening, we pay attention to everything the other person has to say and we listen until they are finished speaking. We do not interrupt. While such intense attention may sound time consuming, it saves time in the long run. Upset persons demand to be heard. Not listening to upset people makes them even more determined to describe the problem. When we listen well, the upset person doesn't need to spend unnecessary time capturing our attention. In addition, good listening communicates caring.

In order to listen well, we need to pay special attention to Channel One, the language channel. Information presented on the language channel provides us with the facts about the upset. We also need to be tuned into Channel Four, the channel that carries feelings. Channel Four helps us gain an understanding of what the upset person is feeling.

Since upset people are generally behaving out of their child ego state, they usually respond warmly to caring parents. Unfortunately, we are more likely to respond as critical parents than as caring parents when dealing with the upset person's child ego state. Most of us have spent long years developing the ability to listen for those things with which we disagree. When we argue with others, our ears seem trained to listen for and point out the holes in their thinking. The other person may have spoken for several minutes and said several things with which we have no argument. But the moment something is said with which we don't agree, it is almost like we are saying, "Aha, I caught you." Success in dealing with upset people requires *listening for agreement.* To agree with another person on some points greatly reduces friction and upset.

In summary, there are three basic ideas to

remember and practice when listening to upset people:

- listen attentively to the whole story from beginning to end

- listen for understanding of feelings as well as of issues

- listen for areas of agreement

Activities for developing listening skills

1) Listen carefully to a television program not only for the content but for all channels of communication. Practice this with a program you usually watch. Do you find any differences in what you observe when you are paying careful attention to all seven channels? Then watch a program that is either new to you or not part of your usual interests. Outline what you observe on each of the seven channels.

2) Ask a friend to help you with this exercise. Have your friend share something about which he or she is or has been upset — perhaps an issue with a spouse, boss, child, or another friend; perhaps a complaint about something annoying. Listen carefully for both the content and the feelings. Then rephrase what you think the person was saying and feeling. Ask your friend for feedback as to how you did. If necessary, continue to refine your rephrasing of the content and

understanding of the feelings.

Empathizing

Empathy is defined as the ability to put oneself in another person's shoes; the ability mentally to identify oneself with another person. When we successfully empathize with someone, we are making appropriate use of our caring parent ego state.

Empathy is *not* minimizing the problem. It is *not* saying, "That's not so bad" or "It could be worse." Nor is it saying, "Oh my gosh, that's awful." Rather than being helpful, awfulizing (as described in Chapter Three) only serves to further upset an already upset person. Empathy is *not* advice. It is *not* telling someone how to solve a problem. And finally, empathy is *not* taking the attention off the upset person and redirecting it to oneself. This is not helpful. In hospital settings, for example, a visitor sometimes attempts to cheer a patient by describing personal illnesses, surgeries, and health issues. The poor upset, ill, and captive patient! Empathy is *not* saying, "So you think *you've* got a problem."

To empathize *is* to listen to another person's complaint or upset feelings without making judgments.

The more we experience the other person's viewpoint, the easier it is to empathize. We need to be able to identify with the feelings of a child when he or she is being teased by playmates; of a friend who is fighting with the boss; of a family member who is upset because we are two hours late arriving home. When we can put ourselves in other people's shoes, we can better understand their upset.

And yet, sometimes things block our capacity to put ourselves in another's shoes. What are some of the things that get in the way of our ability to empathize? There are at least four.

Feeling attacked

Feeling personally attacked can limit our capacity to empathize. When we feel we are being personally attacked, the natural, instinctive response is to mobilize to defend ourselves. We defend rather than listen and empathize. If we believe that in order to understand another person, we also have to agree with them, then there is an even greater likelihood that feeling personally attacked will intrude on our ability to empathize. It is helpful to remember that understanding someone does not necessarily mean agreeing with him or her. In a later chapter we will provide you with some specific self-management techniques that can help you overcome these defensive feelings.

Fear of responsibility

A second factor that can interfere with our ability to empathize with and understand others is our fear that we may be responsible for the upset in some way. To empathize with someone is not the same thing as admitting fault. It is possible to express concern without taking responsibility. We are not suggesting that each of us doesn't sometimes bear some responsibility for another person's upset. It is important, however, to have sufficient information about a problem before rushing in and admitting fault. Below are some statements of problems and several pairs of responses to each problem. Both responses express understanding and concern. One of the responses, however, also takes on more responsibility or fault than is recommended based on available information. Take a few minutes to read through the following six pairs of examples and check the reponse you think is preferable. Remember, we are looking for ways to show concern without taking on responsibility.

1. "I just received your check from the bank marked "insufficient funds'."

    A. "I'm sorry. If there's been a mistake, I'd certainly want to correct it."

    B. "I'm sorry. I'm not usually overdrawn."

2. "Your daughter was very rude to me when I called."

    A. "I'm sorry she was rude. I've tried to teach her good manners."

    B. "I'm sorry you were upset. Is there something I can help you with now?"

3. "You never listen to anything I say."

    A. "I'm really sorry you feel that way. What would you like me to listen to now?"

    B. "I'm sorry. I get caught up in my own thoughts too much."

4. "Where are the decorations for the church social? You were supposed to have them here by now."

    A. "I'll be there with them in an hour. It would concern me if things didn't run smoothly."

    B. "I'm sorry I'm late."

5. "My wife slipped on your steps yesterday and her back is giving her a lot of trouble today."

    A. "I'm sorry. We need new carpeting."

     B. "I'm sorry that your wife isn't feeling well."

6. "You sent the wrong lunch to work with me this
     morning."

     A. "I'm sorry if it wasn't what you expected."

     B. "I'm sorry! I'm usually more careful."

In our opinion, the preferred responses are: 1-A;
2-B; 3-A; 4-A; 5-B; 6-A. Now go back and check to see
if you selected the response that was empathic without
admitting fault. You can practice developing empathy
without admitting responsibility by anticipating people's
complaints and preparing in advance some responses
to these.

Personal insecurity

Insecurity about ourselves, our abilities, our
families, and anything else that is important to us can
also affect our empathizing skills. The more secure a
person feels, the easier it is to lower defenses, to listen,
and to empathize. On the other hand, too much
self-centeredness and self-involvement can lower the
capacity to empathize.

It can be a problem to care too much about oneself
and not enough about the other person and it can also
be a problem to care too much about others and not

enough about oneself.

Limited perspective

Finally, the ability to empathize can be obstructed by having a limited perspective about other people. How can we put ourselves in another person's shoes if we have not had any similar life experiences? If we've always been able to eat everything we wanted to eat without gaining weight, how can we understand what it's like to have a chronic weight problem? If we've always been employed, how can we understand the person who has been out of work? If we lack a frame of reference in which to place a situation, we will be less effective at empathizing.

However, never having experienced something doesn't necessarily mean we are unable to understand it. We can develop empathy around many situations by remembering similar experiences in our own lives and by imagining what it would feel like if we had the other person's problem. We may never have been unemployed, but we can try to imagine the feelings we would have if we had no place to go in the morning, no money coming in, no way to provide for our family, and no sense of productivity. Using our imaginations is an excellent way of improving our ability to empathize with people.

Statement of regret

The opening comment in an empathy statement is a brief statement of regret directed toward the other person's complaint or upset. "I'm sorry you had a bad day." "I'm sorry you are having problems with your mother." "I'm sorry you worried about my being late." Each of these is a statement of regret. You'll notice that blame is not assigned in any of these statements. You have neither said "I'm sorry your mother is so difficult" nor "You really should try to be a more understanding daughter."

When possible, empathy can be more than just the brief statement of regret. It can provide an opening in which to communicate your understanding of the other person's feelings. "I'm sorry you and your mother are having problems. It must be very frustrating when you are trying so hard to be a good daughter."

When people are upset about something, they need some reassurance that their feelings have been acknowledged and understood. Like listening, the power of empathy cannot be overestimated. Many times, the primary request of the upset person is to be understood. We can *always* listen and empathize, even in situations where we cannot meet additional wishes of the upset person. At the least, we can empathize with and understand a person's wish. "I can certainly understand how much you wish you did not need surgery."

> A couple of years ago, I (Pennie) became more than a little disgruntled with the phone company. I was without service for almost a week. Every day when I called, an operator would tell me that service would be restored before 6 p.m. the next day. Finally, on the sixth day when my phone was still not in working order, I rushed next door to use my neighbor's phone, attacking the first operator I reached. After raving and ranting, running out of breath, and wearing thin my vocal chords, I stopped and said, "I don't know why I'm yelling at you. I'm sure you're not responsible for my problem." Graciously the operator said, "It's O.K. lady, if it feels good to yell, go ahead and yell. I don't mind listening."

Activities for developing empathizing skills

1) Observe others when you are out shopping, eating, or participating in a community event. Try to imagine people's lives based on the cues they send. Imagine how they live, where they work, what their relationships are like, and how they feel about different things.

2) We all are involved with people. Whenever you are having a conversation with another person, try to put

yourself in his or her shoes. Think about how you would react to you, if you were the other person.

3) Listen and watch carefully for what you think others are feeling. Notice the little ways in which people let you know what their feelings are. Check to make sure you understand their feelings by saying:

It sounds like you feel_____.

I can understand how you feel when_____.

Are you feeling_____?

Can you share your feelings with me?

Clarifying

There are times when an upset person just needs a sympathetic ear — someone to listen and understand. Situations related to grief are examples of these times. However, while listening and empathizing are necessary, they are not always sufficient. In addition, upset people expect to find a solution to their problem. It is necessary to be clear about the nature of the problem if we are to be successful in helping to resolve it. Consequently, the third ingredient in this formula is the process of clarifying.

Clarifying is just what the word implies: "to make

more clear." Clarifying helps you and the upset person gain a better understanding about the upset feelings, the cause of the upset, and exactly what the problem is that needs resolving. Whereas empathizing is putting yourself in the other person's shoes, clarifying is the process through which *both* parties gain a better understanding of the situation. In order to be helpful, we need to have full knowledge of the upset person's feelings and full knowledge of the content of his/her problem.

It may help to know what clarifying *is not* in order to better recognize what it *is.* Clarifying is definitely *not* evaluating, moralizing, lecturing, or preaching — a fact sometimes forgotten by the eager helper. It is not useful to become critical parents when dealing with an upset person no matter how obviously the upset person may have mismanaged an aspect of his or her life. Critical parents turn upset people into defensive children. The goal in dealing with upset people is to move people into their adult ego state from either their child or their parent state. This phase employs the useful exchange of information. Below we describe five particular behaviors that are helpful in successful clarifying.

Information-seeking

A role we often play in the clarifying process is that of information seeker. We may need more information than we have if we are going to be able effectively to help the upset person. A review of helpful information-seeking skills follows:

1) Paraphrasing and checking for understanding:

Paraphrasing and checking for understanding are valuable communication tools for handling upset persons. Paraphrasing involves repeating our understanding of the *content of the message* in our own words. Checking for understanding involves describing what we think the other person is *feeling* . A clear understanding of both the content of the message and the upset person's feelings is necessary in the successful management of upset. If we behave because of what we *think* another person is saying or feeling, we may be wrong. It is impossible to go wrong by paraphrasing and checking for understanding. The other person may say, "Yes, that's what I meant" or "Yes, that's how I feel," or he or she may say, "No, let me try to explain again." In either case, we have improved our understanding of the nature of the upset.

2)   Open vs. closed questions:

Open questions encourage the respondent to give more than a one-word answer. Open questions are useful for gaining information and for allowing the upset or complaining person to express his or her feelings. Examples of open-ended questions are:

> "Tell me what's bothering you about moving to Minnesota!"

> "What seems to be the problem with our budget?"

> "How haven't I been holding up my end of the family responsibilities?"

When you are clarifying, open questions give you more information than the following closed questions:

> "Do you dislike colder climates?"

> "Are we overdrawn?"

> "Haven't the meals been O.K.?"

As you can see, these closed questions provide much more limited information.

Closed questions encourage brief, specific answers and are useful if you need to elicit specific information. Requests for dates, times, and numbers, as well as questions that can be answered Yes or No are closed questions. Closed questions may be helpful when someone is very upset, is out of control, or has been talking too long. Then, the goal is to help them calm down and gain control of themselves. At such times, closed questions can follow an empathy statement. "I'm sorry you had to wait for me. How long will it take us to get to the theater?"

3) What, when, where, and how vs. why:

Questions that ask what, where, when and how have us seeking information that will be useful in problem solving. "What would you like for dinner tomorrow?" "Where would you prefer I park the car?" "How can we cut down on our spending?" Questions that begin with "why," on the other hand, require explanations and tend to put the upset person on the defensive. When we ask a person why he or she did something, that person, then, looks for a way to convince us that there was a good reason for the behavior.

"How do you think you might earn the money to pay for your speeding ticket?" is a more appropriate question to ask a seventeen-year-old son than "Why were you going so fast?" In phrasing the question this way, the parent communicates disapproval but also understanding of the son's dilemma. In addition to serving a clarifying function, the question focuses on problem solving. We can understand his upset and still share our disapproval. "I know you're upset you got a ticket and I need you to know that I do not expect you to drive fast or recklessly. I love you and want you safe."

It is often the *way* in which questions are asked (Channel Two) rather than what questions are being asked (Channel One) that escalates or reduces the other person's upset. It is important to have your manner convey genuine concern. "What in the world do *you* have to complain about?" is not what we mean by a "what" question. The inappropriate use of sarcasm has upset many a person who started out with only a mild complaint.

Finally, we need to remember that an upsetting incident involves two parties. We are not the only ones who have some responsibility for clarifying the issues. Sometimes our efforts at asking questions produce silence or even more upset. If none of our clarifying questions appear to be helpful, we can ask the upset person to tell us what he or she needs. We can ask, for example, "What would be helpful to you?" This redirects some of the responsibility back to the upset person and removes some of the responsibility from us.

Information-giving

Giving an upset person information is another way of clarifying the problem. For example, when I (Don) rushed to the emergency room with my son who had just broken his arm, and the admitting person began asking for insurance information, my upset escalated. My son's broken arm is a crisis for me even though it is not a crisis for the emergency room personnel. Adding clarifying information to the request would have reduced my upset. "Can I trouble you for your insurance card? It will help us expedite the procedures and get your son's broken arm looked at more quickly." By the way, most people who are upset by health issues are reassured by receiving information.

There are other ways in which information giving is clarifying for an upset person. We overheard a woman in a grocery store complaining to the manager that the milk her son had just purchased was spoiled. She demanded that the manager take back the milk and give her a new half gallon. The manager politely and quietly informed the woman that the particular brand of milk she was returning was the house brand of another chain of supermarkets. Needless to say her behavior changed dramatically. The information was essential to the outcome. As in information seeking, the manner channel is critical in information giving.

The purpose of clarifying is to enable both parties to develop a clearer understanding of the problem or issue. Roles also may need clarifying. Sometimes we are not sure what part the upset person expects us to play in a situation. For example, if a loved one comes home after a bad day at work and complains about the job is he or she asking for an understanding listener, advice about how to handle the boss, or support for leaving the job and looking for a new one?   When dealing with an upset person, it is also important to know whether you are a part of the problem or are just the person to whom the upset person is complaining.

Activities for developing clarifiying skills

1)   As you talk with other people, be aware of the frequency with which you use what, where, when, how and why questions and open/closed questions. Practice eliminating the why questions. Look for new ways to ask for information. Practice asking open questions when you want to help other people express themselves and/or you want lots of information. Practice asking closed questions when you want

specific information or to help the other person be brief or control feelings.   If you are wanting more open communication with your family members, you will find the art of questioning invaluable.

2)   While reading or watching TV be aware of what information you are missing and would like to have. Write down specific questions. Write down information you think would be helpful to share.

3) Paraphrasing content and checking for understanding of feelings are just as critical to clarification as they are to empathizing. Therefore, the empathizing activities also can be used to help develop clarification skills. Paraphrase what you think the other person is saying.   Check for understanding by using empathizing activity #3.

4)   When giving instructions, request that the other person paraphrase the instructions prior to starting the task.

5)   When asked to do any assignment (for example, committee work, planning a family reunion, taking the scouts camping, or a work assignment) make a list of additional information that would help you perform the task. Practice asking your clarifying questions before approaching those who might have the answers.

Problem Solving

After the problem has been clearly identified, solutions can be sought. Problem solving, as mentioned previously, does not include blaming. Blaming assigns the problem to someone whereas effective problem solving requires that the problem be out on the table in front of both parties. Both parties can work together to seek a satisfactory solution. You do not need the answers to the upset person's dilemma in order to be effective in helping solve the problem. You do need, however, some ideas about how to go about the task of finding the answers. Suppose, for example, a member of your church comes to you with a family problem. A son is suddenly acting moody and doing poorly in school. The congregant is certain that drug and alcohol abuse are involved. Rather than being overwhelmed by the task of solving the problem, you only need to have some ideas about how the family can find available options. Even if you know nothing about adolescent drug and alcohol problems, you can help the upset parent by directing him or her to a physician, a local mental health association, alcoholics anonymous, a school counselor, or even the local phone book. Increase your familiarity with your local helping resources. (The United Way in many communities provides a resource book listing all the available resources for a variety of problems.)

Problem-solving abilities can be enhanced by imagination, fantasy, and brainstorming. Use any or all of the following to find creative solutions to sticky problems.

- Think of every possible solution — even those that seem crazy or impossible. Don't evaluate until you've exhausted all possibilities.

- Think of ideal outcomes.

- Think of the worst possible things to do.

- Check out solutions other people have used.

A young couple spent the better part of several weeks fighting over vacation plans. The two unresolved issues were whether to include children and what means of transportation they could afford. Mother didn't want to spend two weeks in the car with the children and Father wanted to include the children but couldn't figure out how to manage five plane fares on their vacation budget. The couple was stuck. Once they began to fantasize the ideal situation, they were able to design a vacation plan that pleased everyone. Mom and Dad drove to Florida, enjoying a week to themselves. The children spent the first week with their grandparents. Both grandparents and grandchildren profited from this special family time. The children then flew to Florida to meet their parents. The two youngest children flew home. The eleven-year-old son enjoyed the privilege of several days alone with his parents on the trip back.

Additional problem-solving strategies

It is better to tell people what we *can* do for them than what we *can't* do.Telling a thirteen-year-old, "You can have six friends over for a pajama party next weekend" is preferable to, "Absolutley no boy-girl parties." The simple skill of using "can do" improves the likelihood of reducing upset.

If it is not possible to meet someone's request, use the word *can't* rather than *won't.* Saying you won't do something indicates you could do it but refuse to do so. Saying you can't suggests it is not possible.

Sometimes it is helpful to ask an upset person what he or she would suggest you do. In other words, return the problem to the upset person. When an upset person becomes responsible for finding the solution, he or she often realizes your dilemma and perhaps even the unreasonableness of the request. The upset person is more likely to accept a solution if he or she has had a role in developing it. If the person continues to be unreasonable, feelings probably have not been effectively addressed. In this case, it is necessary to return to the listening and empathizing stages of the formula. The upset person is not ready for an adult-to-adult transaction.

> When my (Pennie) children were teenagers, they were sometimes upset by the limits I placed on them related to their curfew. Often I would ask them to set their own curfews. Not surprisingly, they would set hours that were agreeable to both of us.

Most upset persons want to know that everything possible is being done to resolve their problem. Listening, understanding and giving them our very best shot at being helpful is what we need to do to handle complaints and upsets satisfactorily.

Activities for developing problem-solving skills

Before you embark on either of the following exercises be certain that you can *identify* the problem. Correct problem identification is essential. If it has more than one part, do the exercise for each part of the problem.

1)   The following is an excellent procedure you can use for a current problem you are trying to solve. The activity can be done individually or can involve several

people.

a) List all possible solutions to the problem. If appropriate, ask others to add to your list. In this stage of problem solving do not evaluate the potential solutions. List everything, even if you are aware of problems in the solutions.

b) Cross unacceptable solutions off the list.

c) Arrange the remaining solutions in order; starting with those you like best and ending with those you like least. This part of the process usually requires that participating problem-solvers are aware of the benefits and costs of each possible solution.

d) Select the top choice and put it to work.

e) Evaluate the solution you have selected after an appropriate time. This is an important step because decisions are more difficult when we believe that once we decide on a course of action we can never turn back or change our mind.

f) If the solution is not working or if it is not helping solve the problem, select another potential solution from your list.

Suppose, for example, your son is upset by the problem of what to do with his life after high school graduation. The above problem-solving process may prove helpful. The list of solutions could include everything he can think of from going to college, to getting various jobs, to joining the military, to lying around doing nothing for a year. Don't forget to have him include even the most absurd possibilities. After eliminating unacceptable options and listing the remaining solutions based on the costs and benefits, he can select a course of action. Choosing one of the options will be easier if he limits himself to a particular time frame. He might decide, for example, "I will take a one-year electrician's training course at the local vocational/technical school. However, at the end of six months, I will evaluate how the course is working for me. If I discover I have little apptitude for, or interest in, becoming an electrician, I will go back to my potential solutions list." Suprisingly, the freedom not to have to stick with an unsatisfactory choice often allows us to try new behaviors and, in the process, to discover new and exciting things.

2)   After you have specifically pinpointed a problem,

imagine the craziest, wildest, most ridiculous solution possible. What , if any, would be the value in such a wild, crazy solution? What would be some of the problems? The goal of this type of problem-solving activity is to help you let your imagination grow in the hopes of generating more creative solutions. We often learn that solutions we thought of as crazy are very workable.

> A woman was complaining about her husband's depression, particularly his lack of energy, his moodiness, and his inability to make decisions. She said she had tried absolutely everything she could think of to help him snap out of it. When she was asked to think of the worst possible thing she could do with him, she thought for several pensive moments. Then she got a lightbulb expression in her eyes. Suddenly she broke out in a grin and said, "I thought of something awful I could do, but now that I think of it perhaps instead of being awful it's the one thing I should have been doing all along but have been too afraid to try. I think I need to confront him more directly about his behavior rather than just tippy-toe around him for fear I'll upset him. Maybe my tippy-toeing has sent him the message that he is truly fragile and unable to do much."

Problems encountered in problem solving

It is not unusual for upset to be the result of the

frustration we feel as we work at solving our everyday problems. Each of us approaches problem solving in a unique way. Some styles work better than others to lessen the frustration.

> In a restroom in the Los Angeles airport, a woman was attempting to obtain some soap from the soap dispenser. Over and over again, she pushed *up* on the lever of the soap dispenser. When nothing happened, she would redouble her attack on the wall-mounted bottle. The sign on the soap dispenser above another sink read "push *down* on handle." In that one brief moment, the woman in the rest room exemplified all the frustration and upset we sometimes experience when we continue to inappropriately attack life's problems, large or small.

People get frustrated and upset when they are working hard at something and still get no results. In the illustration above, it is obvious that people who continue to attack a problem over and over again in the same ineffective way are not as successful in resolving their problems as people who have learned to step back from the problem in order to get a different perspective on possible new solutions. When the woman was unable to get soap from the soap dispenser by pushing up on the handle, she needed to ask herself if she had labeled the problem correctly and, if so, what other solutions were possible. For example, if the soap dispenser was empty, she was attacking the wrong problem. The problem, in that case, would be to find some soap. If there was soap in the soap dish, then the problem was how to get it out. Clearly, pushing up was not the answer. What other possibilities were there—pushing back, pushing down, unscrewing the bottle, etc.? Sometimes we approach a family problem or a personal problem like this woman approached the soap dish. Perhaps we have had the same argument about our spouse's drinking over and over again. We need to step back and ask ourselves, "How can I handle this problem differently since what I am doing is not working?" The purpose of this section is to describe nonproductive patterns of coping with problems and to present more useful approaches to problem handling.

Chronic Complainers

The world is full of people who might best be described as chronically upset about something. Chronic complainers are one example of the chronically upset. Chronic complainers are people who always complain about something. People chronically complain for many different reasons. A few of those reasons are listed below.

- they learned to complain because it was the behavioral style of the family in which they grew up

- they were reinforced in some way for complaining(remember the manipulative child described in Chapter Three)

- they haven't discovered a way to get other people to listen to them and take them seriously

- they are pleading for attention in the only way they know how.

Harry had moved from Houston a year earlier to a town about 100 miles from Chicago. Harry's widowered father lived in Chicago. After the move, Harry began receiving frequent and frantic calls from his father. These calls were filled with complaints about various health problems. Weekends had Harry making hurried trips to Chicago in response to his father's upsetting calls. Within six months, Harry found himself overwhelmed by his father's health complaints. He also began hearing a new set of complaints from his wife, who resented Harry spending all of his weekends with his father in Chicago.

Meeting the demands associated with chronic complaints is not usually the solution to eliminating the problem. The first step (straight out of the formula for handling upset people) is listening. In the case of chronic complaints, the purpose of listening is to understand the real intent of the complaining. In Harry's case his Dad may have been saying, "I'm lonely" or "I'd like to see you." If so, Harry, then, can respond to the true meaning of the complaint. For example, he might try calling his Dad more frequently and just chatting. Or he could say, "I know you wish I could come to Chicago this weekend but that won't be possible. Mildred and I can come up the weekend of August 16th if that will work with your schedule." In this way, Harry would have more control over the scheduling of his visits. Or, he might say, "When you are feeling better, I'll try to get to Chicago so that we can spend a couple of hours together. I'd hate to waste a trip when you're not feeling well enough to visit or do anything." This response helps Harry's Dad to change his behavior (complain less) if he wants to spend time with Harry. When we respond immediately to inappropriate complaints and requests, we are teaching complainers to continue to complain. By listening carefully, we learn to hear the problem underlying the complaint. Then we can focus on teaching the complainer a new and more functional method for getting his or her needs met.

Chronic complaining is sometimes the result of complainers feeling so overwhelmed by their problems that they then overwhelm us with their complaints. A useful technique for handling this kind of upset is what we call *making molehills out of mountains.* Big problems can be overwhelming! Renovating an old house, for example, is a monumental task. Tackling one room at a time subdivides the goal in such a way as to allow the experience of success at shorter intervals. It is easier to focus on the house one room at a time. When dealing with an upset person who is feeling swamped by the problem, help him or her to break it down into manageable chunks.

To further illustrate this point, let's imagine someone has been complaining to you that her spouse finds fault with everything she does. Such marital accusations may feel mountainous to her. After listening attentively, ask this person to focus on just one of the things about which her husband is unhappy — something she, too, would like to change. If she responds that both she and her husband wish she could keep the house cleaner, she is in danger of feeling overwhelmed by that problem alone. We can help her by asking her to identify one household task that she thinks she could manage to accomplish in the next week. The goal of the helper is to help the upset person work on a problem that has high likelihood of turning out successfully.

Just as individuals can feel overwhelmed by their problems, so can whole families feel overwhelmed by problems. Turning mountains into molehills is one way to directly attack this kind of upset.

Our personal attitude toward a complaint influences how we feel about complainers. A complaint is not a personal attack. It is information. A person who is complaining is sharing information with us and values the relationship with us enough to want to work things out. Complaints tells us that the complaining person wishes to continue to interact with us. Where there are no complaints, there are no opportunities for improvement. We rarely hear a person's last complaint. The way to build a better mousetrap or a better marriage is to know what needs changing.

An elderly man came home one night and told his wife of thirty-two years that he had filed for divorce. Absolutely every detail of the divorce had already been planned and executed. The wife was dumbfounded. She had no idea that her husband was so unhappy. Had he complained more and sooner, changes might have been made to help make the marriage more satisfactory for both husband and wife. He left the marriage and with him left any opportunity this couple may have had to improve their relationship.

Finally, some people become chronic complainers about chronic complainers. If you find yourself surrounded by upset people who continually complain to you, you are in danger of becoming a complainer about complainers. It may be time for you to assert yourself and state your limits. You may need to say such things as:

- "I'm sorry but I can't listen any more

- "Unless you really want to work on changing the problem, it doesn't feel fruitful to continue to talk about this."

- "If you can't control your complaining about this, we will be spending less time together."

Confronting people in order to help them to help themselves may feel cruel but it may be helpful for both parties. It is better to state your limits than it is to withdraw, leaving the chronic complainer to ponder the reason for your withdrawal (and, no doubt, the withdrawal of others).

Chronic Worriers

Whereas chronic complainers are upset about present issues, chronic worriers are upset about the possibility of a future problem, the "what ifs." Worrying originates from long-term habit or from a superstitious belief that through worry, one can control the future. Chronic worriers believe that if they give up worrying, they would increase the possibility of their fears coming true. Since worry consumes a great deal of time, giving up worrying would also present chronic worriers with the potential problem of how to fill time previously spent worrying. The following list provides some tips for managing the upset of the chronic worrier.

- Help worriers to turn their worry into planning.
  Use questions like:
  > "If that happened, what would you do?"
  > "What, in your worry, can you control?
  > "How likely is that to occur?"
  > "What would happen if that occurred?"

- Don't dismiss the concerns of the worrier with statements such as "don't be silly."

- Make rational input such as described in Chapter Three.

- Help worriers to restructure their worry. For example, they might keep a worry log or diary to help them get a sense of the scope of their worry. Or they might set aside a certain time of the day for worrying and save all their worries until that special time.

Worriers can also make a list of their worries. The list can help them to sort out :

- Worries they cannot control such as: "What if it rains on the day of the Sunday School picnic? Since they cannot control the weather, worry will not help. But planning will help.

- Worries they can plan for such as: "What will we do if it rains on the day of the Sunday School picnic?" This is the list that worriers can really tackle.

- Worries that are irrational and therefore highly unlikely to happen such as: "What if it rains the day of the Sunday School picnic and after holding the picnic in the community hall of the church, a tornado blows the church away?" The worrier can calculate the odds of such a happening and then decide how much energy to put into worrying. In addition, worriers could plan for those aspects of the worry that planning would help. For example, if there was a very bad storm, what would we need to do?

My Problems Are My Friends

Another category of chronically upset people are those whose longstanding problems have become such familiar companions that they would feel lost without them. "What would I focus on without my problem?" is part of what maintains the problem. The old behaviors that are causing problems have become habits. Despite the fact that the problems are upsetting, it would be hard to know how to act without them. Alcohol counselors recognize that alcoholics need to change their lives in order to overcome their addiction. Likewise, spouses of alcoholics also have to change their lives when the alcoholic stops drinking. They need to learn new roles and behaviors if they are to be successful as the spouse of a nondrinking person. If they have been spending their time being the all-responsible member of the family and their spouse stops drinking and is now able to help share the responsibility, they may need to find new activities to fill time previously spent on family chores. Otherwise, there is always the risk that they will unknowingly sabotage the new nondrinking behavior.

The person chronically upset over a problem that has become an old friend needs help in grieving the loss that change would precipitate. All change, even hoped for change, involves loss. We will be discussing how best to help people cope with loss in Chapter Seven.

In addition to grieving their loss, people who constantly complain about a problem may need help learning new roles and behaviors if they are to be divested of their problem. For example, if the daughter of a bedridden parent has received praise for "being such a good daughter," she may need help finding new roles through which to maintain her sense of value once she no longer has responsibility for her parent. Less time spent on caretaking would require new interests and activities to replace the behaviors that were involved in nursing an aging parent.

Unrealistic Expectations and Unsolvable Problems

Unrealistic expectations are sometimes responsible for people becoming or staying upset. Expectations can be too high, or too low, or they may not match the situation. For example, some parents expect their children always to perform at a very high level. Some parents, frankly, don't care much if their children accomplish anything at all. And some parents place the same expectations on all of their children, never taking into account their different skills and abilities. Each set of expectations involves the potential for disappointment and upset.

Defining a problem in such a way that it is unsolvable is another way in which people maintain or escalate their upset.

- "The problem is I'm getting old."

- "The problem is I'm a woman/man/black/short/tall etc.

- "The problem is my mother never loved me."

Such problems truly are not solvable. When faced with an unsolvable problem, check to see if there is another way to describe it. Rational self-talk, as discussed in Chapter Three, can help to redefine problems in ways that permit solutions. People are less upset when they feel their problems can be solved. When we can take action, we are less likely to feel helpless and hopeless. The unsolvable problems described above can be restated:

- "The problem is my reaction to aging. How can I change my reaction?"

- "The problem is how to hurdle some of the barriers related to who I am."

- "The problem is how to get my needs met now."

Once problems are defined in such ways that solutions are possible, upset is lessened because people can begin looking for solutions.

> Elaine, a bright, attractive woman in her forties, was devastated when her husband of twenty-one years asked for a divorce. After describing some of her husband's stated reasons for leaving the marriage, she sadly announced, "I'm unlovable and will never make a happy life for myself." When pressed for evidence that she was indeed unlovable, Elaine's examples included that she was too neat; that she fussed too much with meals and entertaining; and was, therefore,unlovable.She seemed surprised when a friend imagined a scene in which a man valued her homemaking skills. Looking at the problem in this new way changed Elaine's problem to one of finding people who appreciated her. If Elaine should choose to redefine the problem as "How can I learn to relax some of my perfectionistic standards?" then the solution will lie in her learning some new behaviors.

Upset Created By Errors In Problem Solving

Upset can escalate when people lack appropriate problem-solving skills. Often, in our practice, couples and families arrive for counseling feeling quite upset about their problems. The upset they describe is not related to one specific problem. They have many problems because they have not developed skills for working out solutions. We all have and will always have some problems to face. The ability to cope with our problems and find workable solutions to them is the key to dealing with upset resulting from problems. A number of frequently made mistakes in problem solving follows:

Moving to problem-solving too quickly

In previous chapters we described the importance to the upset person of expressing feelings. What is needed the most is a nurturing parent to listen to the upset child. In fact, being listened to and empathized with may be all the upset person wants or needs. Problem solving would interfere with that need to be listened to and understood. And, even when the upset person has a problem to solve, sharing what is truly troubling him or her may take some time. In solving the first problem the upset person describes, we might be solving the wrong problem. The critical point here is be patient — don't move too quickly to problem solving.

Getting married to one solution

Most decisions are *not* etched in stone. Upset is sometimes related to a belief that once we make a decision, we are forever stuck with it. On the contrary, it is frequently possible to change our minds.

> A young man about to graduate from high school informed his parents that he had no interest in going on to college. He preferred to look for a job. His parents, recognizing that he was bright enough to attend college, tried to insist that college was his only possible choice. Everyone's upset was considerable until the boy's father suggested that the boy try college for one semester. The young man did not have to feel trapped into a choice that might not work and the parents did not have to feel that their son had totally avoided a possible option. Neither parents nor son had to stay married to only one solution.

Leaping too soon to one or two solutions

This mistake in the problem-solving process is closely related to the one above. Sometimes it feels like there will be relief in a quick and easy "fix." But taking the time to brainstorm can be an important part of the process. Looking at many possible solutions improves the odds that we will select a good one. The upset person can then feel more assured that the solution is a good one.

Looking for saviors

Similarly, upset people sometimes think that some one thing is going to be the answer to the problem or to all their problems.

"If only I had more money."

"If I could just get married."

"Moving would solve all my problems."

Solutions in the form of seeking saviors are rarely satisfactory for the long term. The key to the long range management of upset is the development of sound coping skills. We will always have problems. But we can learn a process for handling them. Coping skills are built on a variety of foundations. Examples of these include the practice of problem solving behaviors and an appropriate reliance on religious faith.

Limited search for alternatives

For most kinds of upset, many alternative solutions are possible. Don't limit your search for alternatives. As was suggested earlier in Chapter Five, your imagination can sometimes lead you to a creative solution to a problem.

Analysis paralysis

Some of us tend to spend too much time and energy analyzing problems that don't warrant such detailed attention. Decisions such as what to wear, what to cook for dinner, whether to sell the family business, or whether to leave one's spouse are not all of equal importance. If we worry as much about what to wear as we do about whether or not to divorce, we are likely to be perpetually upset. In dealing with the upset person who is prone to overanalysis, several techniques can be helpful.

- Ask, "What's the worse thing that can happen?" For example, "What's the worst that will happen if you wear something inappropriate to church?"

- Use humor and overexaggeration. "So, you're afraid you wore the same dress to church the last two Sundays? It'd be fun to start a Guiness world's record for number of weeks in a row of church attendance in the same outfit."

- Use assertive straight-talk. Let them know that you think they need to lighten up. (I'm concerned about you. You seem overwhelmed by the problem of what to wear to church. I think it would help you to save your energy for more important issues.)

Lack of implementation

Problem solving needs to result in the implementation of a proposed solution. It is not enough to think of a solution. We have to use the solution after we have developed it. Longstanding or continued upset is sometimes the product of lack of implementation. Committee meetings can often be examples of the problem of lack of implementation. Everyone has ideas and suggestions but no one wants to carry them out.

Teach them to fish

To help and to take over are not the same thing.

A blind friend of ours gets extremely frustrated and upset when faced with new situations. Before he enters new territory, someone always takes him to the new activity and walks him through the steps of the unfamiliar environment once or twice in a practice run. Knowing how to get about in new surroundings is very important to this handicapped person. The navigator friend does an excellent job of teaching self-sufficiency, promoting self-esteem, and reducing the possibility of an upsetting occurrence.

Problems of upset people are not solved by feeling sorry for the person or feeling the need to take over for them.   On the contrary, we are successful in dealing with upset people when we help them get a sense of their own power in a situation. We accomplish this by being in charge of ourselves and by *not* taking over for the upset person.

After the grief of her husband's death subsided, one of my (Don's) grandmother's most pressing problems was how to get herself around town since she didn't know how to drive. My mother did both of them a favor. She provided the money for driving lessons. Despite being over seventy years old, Grandmother mastered driving. It was marvelous for her sense of accomplishment. And my mother never had to feel angry or resentful about being tied down as Grandmother's chauffeur.

Referral

There are times when you cannot help an upset person. Requesting outside input can be very valuable at times like these. Both trained professionals, looking to refer to a more specialized professional, and friends and relatives, looking for objective professional assistance, can profit from making a suitable referral. You will do a better job of referral if you collect respected referral resources from satisfied consumers and do some follow-up work after you have made a referral to see if the upset person has been satisfied with the help he or she has received. As mentioned earlier, your local United Way may be of assistance. Many communities have an information and referral service. The more information you have about referral resources, the more able you will be to make appropriate referrals.

> The husband did not believe in life insurance. He thought investing money for future growth put it to better use. The wife was terrified of being left with small children to support. Her own father had died when she was a child and she had watched her mother struggle financially through the years. The couple was deadlocked — both very upset. The couple's minister was called on to mediate the dispute. Wisely, he referred the couple to a financial planner with no vested interest in selling any particular program. The objective outside input from this professional proved to be most helpful in the resolution of this longstanding and upsetting dispute.

Closing

The closing stage of the formula for handling upset people is very simple. At most it has three parts. First of all, the upset person is asked if there is any other way we can be helpful. Secondly, we thank the person. We can thank them for any number of things: for letting us know of their dissatisfaction; for continuing to stay involved with us; for giving us new information. Finally, some kind of follow-up may be appropriate. Asking how things are going or calling to check on the status of the problem encourages the upset person to continue to be involved with us. One of the nicest stories about follow-up was reported by a workshop participant.

> Bev had driven to a nearby town to return some sheet music. The sheet music was not what Bev expected it to be when she purchased it. Despite being annoyed at having to drive forty miles to exchange her purchase, Bev did feel that the owner of the store had been helpful. By the time she was leaving the store, an icy rain was falling and the weather grew threatening. That evening, safe and snug at home, Bev answered a phone call from the owner of the music store. The owner had been concerned because the weather had become so bad. She was calling to make sure her customer had arrived home safely.

Closing and follow-up can involve small but meaningful bits of symbolic communication. Examples include:

- writing our phone number down and handing it to a grieving friend with instructions that they are to call if they need something

- asking our child with a new and difficult household chore to share his or her progress

- leaving a special note for a loved one after an upsetting or angry interaction.

The closing stage of the process is similar to escorting our house guest to the door. It puts finishing touches on the interaction. It's the way we say, "The End."

Activities for developing closing skills

Practicing in advance of a situation is one of the more helpful techniques for developing closing skills.

a) Think of a difficult closing situation such as:
- telephone conversations
- getting someone out of your office or home
- putting your children to bed
- leaving someone's home
- closing a meeting
- ending a conversation with a teacher, minister or other authority person

b) Select a situation to work on

c) Anticipate what will happen
- use memory of similar past events
- use fantasy of expected events

d) Practice lines to yourself, in a mirror, to a friend, etc. Rework the lines as often as necessary until you feel that you will be successful

e) Practice in the real situation

f) If it didn't go as you hoped, go back to "d"

Now that we have covered the basic behaviors involved in dealing with upset people, we need to spend some time discussing special cases of upset that require sensitive management. Chapter Six describes techniques for dealing with angry people. Chapter Seven will discuss dealing with people who have experienced loss.

CHAPTER SIX
DEALING WITH ANGRY PEOPLE

It had been a long and frustrating day at the office. It seemed to Steve that not one thing had gone smoothly all day long. Suddenly, and catching Steve off-guard, the company comptroller appeared in the main reception area of the department and began yelling at Steve. "How many times have I told you that unless I have your monthly report in my hands on time, I cannot get the projections done on schedule? I am sick and tired of waiting for your stuff. If something doesn't change around here you had better believe that I will complain to somebody who will do something about this situation." Despite Steve's fatigue and frustration, he knew he had to keep his cool. After all, he was in full view of the entire office staff and was dealing with a man who had significant power in the organization.

This chapter is concerned with how to handle angry people. Angry people are upset people. Moreover, *we* become upset people when we find ourselves in the position of having to deal with an angry person. Before we describe the gemeral formula and specific skills and strategies for handling anger, we'd like to discuss two important questions: "What is anger?" and "What causes it?" We are better equipped to cope with angry people if we understand the specific incident that triggered their upset and we may have some success in *preventing* another person from becoming angry if we understand the kinds of situations that are likely to be anger-provoking.

WHAT IS ANGER?

Anger is a feeling! Like other feelings, anger is part of the child in each of us as discussed in Chapter Three. Angry people sometimes act quite childlike, throwing tantrums, raising their voices, and gesturing wildly. However, some angry people will go to great lengths *not* to appear childlike. They will camouflage themselves as critical parents, caring parents, or rational adults. An angry person masquerading as a critical parent, for example, tells us what we *should* have done or *ought* to be doing. This kind of angry person symbolically points a finger at us and while shaking it in our face says such things as:

> "You should be home more. You spend more time working and socializing with your friends than you do at home with your family." (Translation: "I'm angry and hurt that you don't want to spend more time with me.")

Angry people sometimes pretend to be caring parents. These children in nurturing parent disguise are passively angry rather than attacking directly. It's not unusual for their tone to be sarcastic and for them to treat the objects of their anger as stupid children who lack the skills, knowledge, or motivation to be helpful.

> "Dinner isn't ready because I was certain that you'd be too busy to call and tell me you'd be late. I certainly didn't want your dinner to be cold when you *finally* came home." (Translation: "I'm angry that you are late getting home.")

Finally, angry people sometimes present themselves as quite cool and rational. Don't be fooled by super rational angry people. They too are wolves in sheep's clothing — angry people in their child ego state masquerading as adults. They may sound adultlike on Channel One, but Channels Two and Three invariably expose the angry child underneath.

> "Let me try and explain the importance of your getting home from work at a reasonable hour. The children are hungry. They need your attention. And there are household tasks to be done." (Translation: I am angry that you aren't home sooner.")

Emotions other than anger sometimes masquerade as anger. People who are worried, frightened or bereaved may appear to be angry. The anger helps to protect them from feelings of excessive vulnerability.   It is important to recognize the vulnerability in the upset person's anger. If we respond to them as if they are really angry, we will have failed their greater need. We will say more about this later.

Responding to the Angry Child Ego State

We continually need to remind ourselves that angry people approach us out of their child ego state. Realizing this, we can make two important responses: *the caring response* and *the rational adult response.*

People frequently make two mistakes in dealing with anger. The first is to respond to the child in the angry person as a critical parent rather than a caring one. The second mistake is to move directly to adult, bypassing the caring parent altogether. Let's look at some possible responses from the person late getting home from work to the spouse who is angry.

Mistake #1 (Critical response. No caring; no rationality):
"Why should I bother to hurry home? Dinner's never ready anyway."

Mistake #2 (Rational response. No caring):
"When the boss asks me to stay late and work on a project, I don't have a choice if I want to get ahead. And we could use the money a raise would bring."

Appropriate Response (Caring parent and adult):
"I know you wish I could get home earlier. It's tough to be the first one home after work. What can I do to help now?"

As in complaint handling, it is necessary first to understand the person's anger and then work toward resolving the problem. More on this when we get to the formula.

THE ROOTS OF ANGER

Anger is the result of many factors, including the triggering situation, past experience, and individual responses to experience. There are, however, certain situations that predictably lead to anger. As was mentioned in Chapter One, anger is sometimes the result of inappropriate handling of a minor complaint. In cases like these, people are not initially angry but become angry because of something we have either done or failed to do. Obviously, this type of anger is preventable. Positive contact skills and mastery of the complaint-handling formula are invaluable. Other triggers for anger are more complex. Understanding what creates anger in another person is often helpful in planning both preventative strategies and in deciding how to handle anger once it occurs. In addition to secondary upset created by poor complaint handling, there are seven other triggers for anger that we will discuss. Let's look at each of these and at strategies for preventing or managing them.

Dependency

To feel dependent is to feel we need something over which we have no control. Whatever it is that we need, we feel we are unable to provide it for ourselves and we are dependent on someone or something else to meet that need for us. Issues of dependency and control are closely related. When we can't meet our own needs, we have little control over how those needs get addressed. This lack of control makes us angry or, at best, ambivalent.

Examples of the link between dependency and anger are manifold.

- We need the services of public utilities. We feel utility companies control the costs. We feel dependent and often angry.

- Someone is providing our financial support. We feel dependent. We feel controlled and, therefore, angry. Or we may feel ambivalent. Even if we like being supported, we hate feeling dependent and controlled.

- We have damaged merchandise. The store controls the outcome of the complaint. We experience angry feelings anticipating that our need to return the merchandise may not be met.

- We're in a hurry to have lunch. We've ordered our meal and are waiting for our food. We feel dependent on the cook and server to get us out on time. We become irritated and, if we have to wait too long, angry.

People experiencing feelings of dependency and anger can, of course, manage their own feelings by reminding themselves of the behavior that is in their control. They often can discontinue doing business with those whose goods or services are inadequate. They can choose to work toward financial independence. They can switch long distance phone service, turn down their air-conditioners, insulate their homes, carry a sack lunch, etc. Any steps they take to feel more in control and less dependent help them to manage their own anger.

But how do we handle the angry dependent person who is already out of control? When dealing with those who are feeling angry as a result of dependency, we can do those things that encourage them to recognize the extent of their own control over the situation. For example, we can give them limited choices. Utility companies do this when they give customers a choice between regular monthly billings or average monthly billings. Similarly, some stores offer customers a choice of credit or new merchandise when customers return damaged products. Limited choices are available in personal situations, too. An adolescent child may be given the choice of a monthly allowance or a weekly allowance as a solution to money matters. The child who is angry at bedtime can be given a choice about going directly to bed at 8:30 or getting into bed at 8:15 and being read to for fifeteen minutes before bedtime. A spouse who expresses irritation about lack of attention can be asked what in particular would help him or her to feel appreciated. The important point here is that giving people choices is very useful in bypassing or reducing anger. The feeling of having no choices can provoke anger.

The other key to dealing with anger triggered by dependency is the obvious one — helping others to become more independent. Many situations are ripe for us to share information or teach skills. As parents, for example, all of us have a responsibility to teach our children those things that will promote their growth into independent adults. Obviously the child who can't tie his or her own shoelaces has more opportunity to feel angry toward a busy parent than one who has the skill to tie the laces and run out to play. The adolescent who earns his or her own spending money and therefore earns the right to spend part of it as he or she sees fit is less likely to feel angry at parents than the adolescent who has to ask permission for every purchase.The more we teach and train our children, the less dependent and the less angry they feel. The ultimate goal of parenting is to develop our children into self-sufficient adults.

Authority

Authority issues can trigger anger. Either too much or too little structure and direction can be problematic. Imagine for a moment giving a child a chore such as cleaning out the garage. The highly authoritarian person says, "This is what you will do. This is exactly when you will do it. This is exactly how you will do it." There can be no deviation. The possibility of having to deal with an angry, upset child out of this orientation is high. As in dependency issues, over-directed people feel out of control and without any choices. In addition, highly authoritarian people often provoke anger in those they are directing as much because of their manner as because of their requests. People get more upset over "how" directions are given than they do over "what" directions are given. Most of us respond better to requests than to orders.

On the other hand, upset and angry reactions may also result from incomplete or unclear directions for performing a task. The less skilled the person is who will carry out the task, the more frustrated he or she will become if there are insufficient guidelines. New tasks, in particular, need to be well explained. The child who has never cleaned the garage needs both instruction and positive support until he or she has developed the necessary new skills.

Frustration and anger can be prevented by matching your authoritativeness and your directiveness to the situation. The capable, self-motivated person, carrying out a familiar task, probably thrives when left alone. The inexperienced person, executing an unfamiliar task or a brand new activity, needs more detailed instruction and closer supervision. The concept of matching the amount of direction you provide to the situation is useful to the parenting process and to any supervisory situation, including the supervision of volunteers. Small children and children mastering new situations require firmness and direction. Older children, adolescents, and children familiar with a particular situation need a more democratic parenting style. Likewise, the new worker needs more direction than the employee who has been doing the job for a while. In a recent consultation with a Girl Scout administrator, it became clear that several of her new volunteer troop leaders were floundering because of lack of direction. This administrator prided herself on her ability to leave her volunteers alone. We helped her to see that she needed to be more specific with these new volunteers who not only lacked the know-how to perform their function but lacked confidence as well. The important point to remember is to adjust your parenting style to match the needs of the child or your supervisory style to match the needs of the person whom you are supervising. In all situations, you are well advised to maintain Channel Two, manner, at an appropriate level and to vary Channel One, your verbal directiveness, to match the person with whom you are dealing.

Unclear limits

Observe people in an unclear situation and before long you will see their frustration escalate into irritation and eventually anger. Our favorite example of this took place at a conference several years ago. The registration process had registrants searching confusedly for a registration line. When the line was finally discovered, a forty-five minute wait ensued. Believe it or not, when registrants reached the front of the line, they were given a registration form and told to fill it out and then go to another, equally long line. We think you can imagine the level of anger with which the conference planners had to cope.

Prevention is the key to handling anger created by unclear limits. In any situation, put yourself through the paces of those who will be in it — the new volunteer, the customer, the trainee, the participant, the student, the child, etc. Look to see what limits and boundaries are necessary. Specific instructions, clearly posted signs, and well spelled-out rules are useful for clarifying limits. Telling children what is expected of them as well as what will happen if they don't meet expectations and then carrying through demonstrates setting clear limits and boundaries.

Checking to be sure a patient knows where to check in, where to wait, how long he or she can expect to wait and perhaps even what will happen to him or her once in the doctor's examining room can do much to prevent anger and upset. Checking physical territory to outline limits and boundaries and helping others to define psychological limits and boundaries are necessary parts of the process.

While traveling in Florida I (Pennie) got viciously sick from what turned out to be a "bad" oyster. Having previously noticed a walk-in family emergency center, I hurried back to it in the hopes of getting some quick symptom relief. This clinic did a superb job of clarifying limits; an excellent stance for those dealing with sick people. Signs told you exactly where to go and what the payment policy was. The receptionist made a clear statement about how long I'd wait. The nurse who took some blood and urine samples was precise in expectation setting, instructing, and in letting me know it would take fifteen minutes to get the results. She asked if anyone was with me so that she could go out to the waiting room and let that person know I was being detained for lab work. The doctor gave me written instructions for diet and medication and asked me to call if I had further questions. This kind of clarity is excellent for reducing possible points of concern or bewilderment that so frequently lead to anger and upset.

Complexity

The more complex a situation is, the more opportunity there is for something to go wrong and, therefore, for people to get angry. When complexity is the cause of anger, simplification is the prevention or the cure. A case in point is the switch by many banks and airlines from multiple waiting lines to a single feeder waiting line. Customers' exasperation mounted when they observed other lines moving more rapidly than the one in which they were waiting. This procedural simplification from multiple lines to one single line helped both customers and customer service personnel by cutting down on upset.

Similarly, simple requests, directives, and rules help deter family conflict. Long complex explanations about why the children need to be in bed by eight o'clock are not necessary. Overexplaining, one aspect of complexity, creates more upset and anger than it reduces. "It is bedtime" is the simplest directive to give a child.

Scanning the other person's channels and being responsive to what you observe is an excellent approach for preventing upset in potentially complex situations. If you see people wandering about with confused expressions, assume they are unclear about what to do or where to go. Asking "Can I help you find something?" may prevent a bewildered person from becoming an angry one. Sometimes you can see frustration mounting as you attempt to give complex instructions to someone. When this is the case, a switch in tactics is advised. Jot down instructions. Walk the person through the steps or take care of the process yourself. Any time a complex situation can be simplified or broken down into a series of less complicated steps, you enhance your chances of preventing unnecessary anger.

Prior Unresolved Conflict

Another cause of anger is prior unresolved conflict; anger about something that happened in the past which was not satisfactorily resolved. In marriages, for example, we may find ourselves bewildered by an angry spouse for whom some small incident triggered old feelings related to a difficult relationship with his or her parents. People may get angry at an insignificant slight because an old wound has never healed. Perhaps they are still stewing about a thoughtless remark we made at last year's Thanksgiving dinner.

Helen complained that her daughter-in-law seemed edgy and angry whenever they were together. After noticing that family get-togethers were continually being affected by the daughter-in-law's sour disposition, Helen decided to have a talk with her daughter-in-law about this problem. What surfaced from their conversation was the daughter-in-law's long-held angry feelings because Helen had objected to her son's marriage ten years earlier. This old anger toward her mother-in-law had never been resolved and was damaging the current relationship.

When anger is the result of prior unresolved conflict, then it is appropriate to surface the old conflict in an attempt finally to get resolution. Helen, in the example above, is beginning this process. It is obvious that Helen and her daughter-in-law will have to work out these old feelings from ten years ago if they are ever going to enjoy their relationship.

Communcation Problems

Anger is sometimes the unpleasant result of a communication problem. What is actually sent and then actually received in a conversation can resemble "two ships passing in the night." When you suspect that a communication problem is the source of escalating anger, clarify the situation by using clarifying questions, paraphrasing, and checking for understanding as outlined in Chapter Five. Using the dual skills of asking clarifying questions and paraphrasing helps you focus on the content of the sender's message. Checking for understanding allows you to focus on what the sender is feeling.

> "It sounds like this volunteer job is taking much more of your time than you anticipated. You seem understandably upset about it."

> "You feel I am unfair in setting your school-night curfew at 10 o'clock and wish that it could be later."

If you suspect that the other person is having trouble getting your message, you can request a paraphrase or a check for understanding.

> "I want to be sure you understand the issues I'm raising. I know we talked about a lot of different things tonight. Share with me what you think I'm requesting with regard to how the family makes vacation decisions?"

This is a better strategy than being furious because your requests have been ignored and the other person says he or she didn't realize you were making a request.

Conflict of Interest

Finally, anger is often the result of a conflict of interest. Your spouse wants Chinese food for dinner;

you want Mexican. The church youth choir wants their annual trip to be a ski vacation; the choir director prefers a musical tour. Different interests with mutually exclusive positive outcomes can become fertile soils for angry disputes.

Situations involving a conflict of interest are challenging. There are many different ways to try to resolve conflicts of interest. Each strategy can be useful, but it also can be abused. Obviously, in handling conflict situations, the goal is to select the strategy that stands the best chance of successfully resolving the problem. A description of five conflict resolution strategies, along with a discussion of the benefits and costs of each strategy, follows. Some of these strategies will be discussed in more depth when we present the formula for handling upset persons.

The conflict resolution stance of *competing*, a stance where one party wins and one party loses (a win/lose situation) can result in the short-term winner becoming the long-term loser.

> A quilted raincoat was returned by the cleaners with the fabric looking like an overwashed mattress pad. It was clear that the cleaner had mistaken it for a washable garment and inappropriately laundered rather than dry cleaned it. The cleaner felt the customer

should have specifically designated the coat to be dry-cleaned and refused to compensate the customer. The angry customer switched cleaners and has been a faithful customer of the new cleaners for thirty-eight years. For the last twelve or more years, the customer's grown children have also used their mother's recommended cleaners. Who won?

Win/lose strategies are not recommended when you are aiming for a long-term, healthy relationship. A competitive conflict resolution strategy, therefore, is best used when your aim is to have the other party change his or her behavior in the future or leave the relationship. If, for example, you decide that the only way you are willing to maintain your marriage is if your spouse stops drinking, then you may choose a confrontational, win/lose tactic. If there is only one acceptable bookkeeping method for the women's auxilliary, the newly elected treasurer may have to choose either to use it or to resign from office.

In an *accommodating* conflict resolution stance, you choose to lose and let the other party win. In general, use accommodating when you sense that the outcome is very important to the other party and/or when you feel that your current losses will be outweighed by future gains. Agreeing to go on a ski vacation when you had dreams of sunning on the beach in Florida is an example of accommodating. Perhaps vacation plans are more important to your spouse than they are to you. Or, you may decide that a happy spouse who acts lovingly while on vacation is more important than warm weather. The future gains may not be forthcoming if your spouse is grumpy the entire week. Accommodation can be relationship building. However, what usually does not work are relationships in which one person does all the accommodating. Eventually, that person is almost sure to tire of the role.

Compromising is a third strategy for resolving a conflict of interest. In compromising nobody wins all and nobody loses all. It is a strategy based on the philosophy that half a loaf is better than none. Compromising is best used when the two parties have mutually exclusive goals. It often forces the opposed parties to ask for more than what they want, knowing they will have to settle for less. The sale and purchase of residential property is a good example of this. The goals of the two parties are mutually exclusive. The buyer wants top dollar; the seller wants to pay as little as possible. Both state a dollar figure more extreme than what they anticipate settling for. In fact, if a seller takes our first offer, we worry that we offered too much.

The cost in compromising is that neither party is totally satisfied. Sometimes both sides feel as if they have lost. If you end up skiing one winter and sunning the next, one of you may feel cheated during every vacation.

Interests may conflict, but not all conflicts of interest have mutually exclusive goals. More often than not, goals are similar for both parties. For example, the spouses who couldn't decide between a Chinese or a Mexican dinner may have had mutual goals in wanting to get away from the children for an evening and in not wanting to cook and clean up. Two volunteer youth group leaders may be in conflict about what activities to implement. But they will probably be in agreement in their desire to keep the kids involved and active. When conflicting parties focus on their goals rather than on particular alternatives they can *collaborate*. Collaboration is a win/win strategy. The needs of both parties are met. It involves finding mutually acceptable solutions that help both parties to feel successful. The earlier illustration of the family who solved their vacation dilemma by combining driving and flying exemplifies the value of collaboration.

One drawback to collaboration is that it can be time consuming because it often requires a lengthy problem-solving process. And collaboration may be difficult if disagreeing parties cannot agree on goals.

A final conflict resolution strategy is *avoiding*. Avoiding means ignoring the problem. Avoiding strategies are valuable when people need to pick the issues worth fighting over rather than fight over everything. Avoidance is a "peace at all costs" maneuver. It is best used as a strategy of choice when there will be little damage if the conflict is left unattended and where there is a greater positive than negative outcome from not solving the disagreement. Imagine, for example, that you have just reprimanded your son. As he leaves the room, you hear him muttering some grumpy words under his breath. Avoidance may well be the strategy of choice. You want him to be sure to focus on the issue for which he was reprimanded. If you refocus his attention onto being grumpy or muttering a naughty word, you risk fighting over the wrong issue.

An avoiding stance can be problematic though. Avoidance may leave one or both of the conflicting parties unsatisfied with the outcome. Hostility can build up over time, and the eventual conflict may be more difficult to deal with than the avoided conflict. We often call this "the straw that broke the camel's back" syndrome. Avoiding may be a cop-out rather than a strategy if people choose to avoid because they are afraid of the other person's anger or have no skills for problem resolution. Avoiding should not be the inevitable outcome of not knowing what else to do.

All conflict resolution stances have some plusses and some minuses. Each of us needs a broad range of skills for settling conflicts of interests. Practice using all the strategies. Match your strategy to the situation.

THE FORMULA FOR HANDLING ANGER

Once we have some idea of what anger is and what causes it, we are ready to think about a process for defusing anger in other people. The formula for dealing with anger uses the same basic five ingredients as the complaint-handling formula: listening, empathyzing, clarifying, problem solving, and closing. When confronted by an angry person, you use these ingredients in a formula that can be broken down in the steps listed below.

Listening

Listening involves all the skills and behaviors discussed in Chapter Five — only even more so. The higher the level of the upset, the harder it is to listen. In dealing with angry people, we really have to work at listening. Listen for the content, the feelings, and those things with which you can agree. Listen with your caring, understanding parent state and your rational adult state. Listen without your critical parent state, without personalizing, and without counterattacking. Cover your bases by getting information. Cover your hot buttons by not being drawn into an argument. And cover your rear by not putting yourself into positions you'll later regret.

Acknowledging Feelings

Acknowledge that the other person is angry. Do *not* try to talk him or her out of feeling angry. Simply understand what the person is experiencing.

Agreeing

State areas of agreement. This requires a totally different mindset from the one that most of us have learned to use in upset interactions. It means that we are not listening to catch the other person when they exaggerate, get confused, or overreact. Rather, we are listening for those things with which we can agree.

> After a particularly difficult day of training, we decided to reward ourselves with a long, leisurely, and expensive dinner in one of the better-known restaurants in the area. When a costly seafood dish arrived at the table boasting only two shrimp and two scallops, our anger immediately escalated. Don said "No, no way. There are only two small shrimp and two scallops in this dish. I am not going to accept this meal at the price you are asking." The waitress handled herself beautifully. Using the principle of stating areas of agreement she said, "I understand your upset, sir. I know you were expecting more seafood in your serving. Let me return your plate to the chef and see what we can do. Turning to Pennie, she asked, "May I take your meal to the kitchen and keep it warm so that you will both be able to enjoy your meal together?"

The above waitress could have just as easily focused on how poorly we were behaving, how we were the first people to complain, how expensive shrimp and scallops are, or, as was once the case for us in another restaurant, she could have said, "If you could afford it, you wouldn't be complaining." Instead she understood, agreed, and was appropriately appreciated through a generous gratuity.

By the same token, if there is a family dispute over the equitable use of the family car, at the least there can be agreement over the goal that everyone in the family needs some sort of transportation. When all else fails, we can always agree to disagree.

After you have listened, understood, and stated areas of agreement, you may find that before you can move to a problem-solving mode you need more information. As was suggested in Chapter Five, clarifying involves asking neutral, factual questions from your adult state to the angry person's adult state.

Getting Agreement on the Problem

When you are satisfied you have sufficient information, restate the problem in your own words.

> My (Don's) daughter came in an hour and a half late from a school activity. She came in looking like she'd been having a grand time and announced that the group decided to go for pizza after the school play. The response of an angry parent quickly deflated her mood. Finally she said: "I don't think 10:30 is an unreasonable hour." "Neither do I," I answered. "I'm upset because I didn't know where you were and I was worried. I am angry because you didn't call and tell me you'd be late. I expect you to call when you will be later than agreed upon."

In this case my daughter and I did not initially agree on the definition of the problem. I was angry because I was worried and upset that something might have happened to my daughter. My daughter was upset because she thought I was saying that she could not stay out till 10:30 or could not go out with her friends for pizza. It was important to get some agreement on the problem. We eventually agreed that the problem was one of someone being later than expected. Everyone must agree on what the problem is if there is to be a solution. Otherwise, we may argue about and solve the wrong thing. Sometimes defining the problem is the hardest part of the process.

Finding Solutions

A simple phone call was the agreed upon solution for future situations in the scenario described above. But many possible solutions could have been listed before selecting a mutually acceptable one.

1) call if you are going to be late

2) a one-hour grace period

3) come home first and ask for permission

4) no more curfews

5) no exceptions — get home on time

6) check with friends before you leave and make sure you are clear about plans

7) grounded for a specified period of time to teach her a lesson — will be grounded for future violation

8) stop going out with friends, etc.

For some simple problems we quickly compute the possible solutions, almost unconsciously, and then select an appropriate one. For more complex problems, we may list the possible solutions internally, verbally, or in writing. When dealing with angry people, it is often wise to problem solve together; agreeing first on the problem, identifying possible solutions, and then agreeing on one solution. That solution is then implemented. In some situations, the selected solution can be evaluated at a predetermined time. If it is not working, another solution is selected and implemented. This problem-solving process was described in detail in Chapter Five.

Closing

"Is there anything else I can do?" "Are you feeling satisfied at the outcome?" "If you have any further difficulty, please call." "Here's my card." "Let me jot down my name and number for you in case you need anything else." These are all early closing remarks. If you truly believe that the sharing of upset, angry feelings provides useful feedback and indicates a wish to continue the relationship, you can put the icing on the cake by using your personal variation of the following statement:

> "Thank you for letting me know that you were angry (upset, dissatisfied, etc.). I certainly want to keep things straight between us. When I know what the problem is, we have a better chance of solving it."

EIGHT HINTS FOR HANDLING ANGER

Specific behaviors work well in handling angry people and can be useful when applied at various stages of the formula. The person who successfully deals with angry people has mastered the appropriate use of these eight behaviors. Several of these helpful hints have also been described elsewhere in the book.

1) *Communicate confidence and composure.* You need to be in control of yourself since the angry person frequently is not. Your composure is reassuring to both of you.

2)   *Ask for information.* Your goal is to move the angry person from a child ego state to an adult ego state. When in a problem-solving mode, it is more difficult to stay angry.

3)   *Use "I" messages.* If you must talk about the issues as they relate to either of you, use "I" messages. An "I" message is a statement that puts things in terms of how they effect you rather than the other person. "I" messages keep you from placing blame, whereas blaming only fuels the fire of an angry person. "*I'm* sorry, but *I* am unable to allow your friends to drink beer in our home," is a more appropriate response to a teenager's request than, "You and your friends can't drink here and *you* are being irresponsible to even ask."

4)   *Depersonalize angry interactions.* Remind yourself that sometimes angry, upset people are just unloading on you. They do not mean everything they say. At such times they are generally not angry at you, but are angry at the situation.

5)   *Aim for a mutual definition of the problem.* State the problem. Remember that symbolically, your goal is to place the problem on the table between you and the angry person rather than assume the problem belongs

personally to either one of you. "It seems we are having a hard time deciding on a reasonable weeknight curfew" is preferable to "You are making unreasonable demands." The problem is deciding on the curfew, not someone's unreasonableness.

6) *Give people choices.* Angry people feel out of control. If they are given options, it helps them to see that they have some control. We admire the way one of our friends permits her children to experience choice around some of the tasks they hate to do. Many times we've smiled to ourselves as she's asked, "Do you want to set the table now or wait until the next commercial?"

7) *Hold firm assertively.* When you are doing all you can do, it is not necessary to back down or to raise your own anger level. "I'm sorry that my traveling upsets you. My job requires occasional travel and I am going to be out of town a day or two a month." Long explanations, apologies, outrage, or anger are not needed.

8) *Praise yourself.* Remember that dealing with angry people is hard work. You will not always handle everything skillfully, but you are trying hard and working to be more effective. Take a moment to pat yourself on the back.

TEN TECHNIQUES FOR HANDLING THE VERY ANGRY PERSON

Most of us have fearfully faced someone whose overwhelming anger violates the possibility for normal communication.   While this book is not a crisis management primer, it is important to stress that there are limits to what any of us is expected to tolerate from angry, out of control people. We should not maintain communication with the profane, verbally obnoxious, or abusive person. You are always free to draw the line when your sensibilities have reached their limits. Safety is absolutely a primary consideration in the face of physical danger; your safety, the safety of others, and the safety of property. People safety is always more important than property.

Uncontrollable anger is rare. Anger is a normal feeling and is less likely to get out of control when it can be appropriately expressed. We'd like to share some specific strategies for you to use in order to help others maintain or regain control of their anger. Select the strategy or strategies based on each situation. Again, practice is the key.

1)   *Soft to hard.* This technique is synonymous with the last of the six principles for handling upset people

discussed in Chapter One. Respond to angry people at the lowest confrontational level possible. This may mean anything from repeating a person's name three or four times to calling the police or security guard. The point is to match the intervention to the level of anger — not to use a heavier hand than is necessary.

2) *Personalize.* Using a person's name is another technique for dealing with angry people. It is easier to behave badly when you think you are anonymous. Some people prefer to get angry over the phone rather than face-to-face in order to remain anonymous. Names remind angry people that you know who they are. Names are also safe words to use. If someone is yelling at you, you can always say his or her name several quick times in succession to interrupt, "Ginny, GINNY, GINNY." When we don't know the person's name, we can use Sir, Ma'am, or Miss; "Sir, SIR, SIR."

3) *Off feet and away from others.* No one needs an audience when interacting with an angry person. Spectators cause all of us to feel that we need to win in order to save face. Your first goal is to get the angry person away from others and then, if possible, off his/her feet. It is more difficult to yell when you are sitting down.

An agitated client entered the waiting room of our office and began demanding to see a particular counselor, Dr. S. She was talking in loud, boisterous tones and standing over the receptionist in a menacing fashion. Her behavior was upsetting to those in the waiting area as well as to the receptionist. Noticing an empty office a few feet away, the receptionist asked the client to follow her. She grabbed a pad and pencil from her desk on the way. As they walked toward the office the receptionist said "I'll have you wait for Dr. S. in here. Let me get your name so that I can let her know you need to see her."

4) *Yes . . . and.* Yes . . . *but* is a response many of us are familiar with. When we hear, "yes...*but,*" we are prepared to hear a qualified, and therefore, watered down "yes."

> John: "I'm angry that you go out with your women friends after work every Friday. I would like occasionally to celebrate the end of the work week together."

> Jane: "O.K., *but* just once in a while because it's important to me to maintain my relationships with my female friends."

We propose switching to yes . . . *and. And,* rather than *but,* doesn't qualify your agreement. It maintains the agreement full strength while clarifying it.

Jane: "O.K., let's work out a mutually satisfactory schedule so that we can have time together *and* I can maintain my relationships with my friends."

5)   *Match and move.* Sometimes it is a mistake to maintain our cool while other people are practically blowing smoke out their ears. Our calmness seems or looks phony to them and only serves to infuriate them further. When this appears to be the case, we suggest a strategy called "match and move." If the other person is yelling, yell back, but do so with control and then quickly begin to move down the anger scale in terms of intensity.

> Harriet's sixteen year-old son was beside himself over having to mow the yard before he could go to the football game. He worked himself into a screaming fit. When Harriet tried to reason with him, he couldn't hear her over his own rage. Finally Harriet screamed "Shut up, sit down, and listen." Once she had his attention, she quickly lowered her volume and changed her tone as she briefly restated the rule and her expectations.

6)   *What else.* Our spouse, red-faced and breathing hard, is barraging us with a barrelful of anger. His or her angry shots are at everything from the way we handle the children to the way we spend money, to how we look, to our behavior at parties. Once you have

acknowledged that he or she is very upset, ask him or her to be specific about gripes. Continue to ask if there is anything else that is problematic until he or she is out of complaints and out of steam. Engaging the rational adult state helps other people to gain control of their feelings. Asking others to list all their complaints is also a statement of our willingness to work things out. And frequently the real complaint does not surface first. It is the third or fourth item on the list. If we don't bother to ask "what else," we sometimes end up arguing over or problem solving about the wrong thing. In the process of asking a very angry person to list all his or her gripes, the angry person will discover that the list is finite, perhaps much less extensive than was originally thought or felt. We can't stress enough the importance of this tactic and how different it is from defensively arguing with each point. Using the strategy of "what else" requires lots of practice and the lowering of personal defenses.

7) *Beating to the punch.* My (Pennie's) son was a master of this anger-defusing technique. When he would do something that infuriated me, he would wisely approach me with, "Mom, you're gonna kill me. I'd be mad, too, if I were you." It's very difficult to

maintain an angry aggressive stance with a person who's admitting fault. When you're at fault and you both know it, try the "beat to the punch" approach. A similar stance has you simply agree with the upset person. "I'd be upset too if . . . " You can always agree with a person's wish. "I know you wish that this had not happened."

8) *Do what they're already doing.* When you feel that you will not be able to change how the angry person is behaving, tell him or her to do what he or she is already doing. "Go ahead and scream." "Let me get you a tissue." "Stand right here while I find the manager." "You can continue to pound the desk, but I am leaving."

9) *Ignore/Deny.*   People who continue to make unreasonable demands forfeit the right to be taken seriously. In such cases you have the right to ignore their demands or to deny them. There is a time to say "I'm sorry, I do not believe you." We also may choose to ignore an occasional off-color word that slips into the speech of the upset person.

10) *Same song — Different verse.*   People who continue to make demands or carry on unnecessarily should be told repeatedly that their demands will not be met or that they will not get their way by continuing to

persist. Continue saying "No" in as many ways as you choose until your point is understood. Do *not* reward the other person's persistence by giving in. Children who get rewarded by persisting until they get their way continue to be persistent, manipulative, and hard to live with.

We have shared a number of strategies for coping with angry, upset people. We believe that only a small percentage of those with whom you interact will escalate to that very angry stance. More commonly, people who are handled positively rarely become upset or, if they have complaints, those complaints can be handled before anger erupts. For that small percentage of really angry people, however, you can achieve success by practicing all of the strategies outlined in this chapter. Mentally rehearse in your head. Think through how you will respond if faced with various problematic situations. Play out different approaches in front of a mirror or with a friend or family member. Finally, use these strategies in real life situations. Practice is important!

CHAPTER SEVEN
DEALING WITH LOSS

Most of Harry's friends knew that he had made a hurried trip to the Mayo Clinic the previous week. Harry had been experiencing symptoms that were frighteningly similar to those associated with colon cancer. Now, as Harry's friends mingled and chatted at the church social, they were uncomfortably aware of Harry's wife Martha who looked depressed and fearful. When she was asked about Harry's condition, Martha dabbed at her eyes while explaining that Harry had definitely been diagnosed as having cancer. The doctors felt that because the cancer was so far along, Harry would probably not live long. No one at the social knew what to say to Martha.

In this chapter, we will be discussing how to deal with people who are grieving. Grief is the natural response to loss and unwanted change. The discomfort that Harry and Martha's friends felt in finding themselves face to face with Martha was typical and to be expected. Most of us are unsure about how to behave when we are faced with people who are struggling to cope with loss or unwanted change. To suffer a loss is to suffer a deprivation. Loss is a broad term that includes many things, from a lost promotion to a lost sporting competition, to the death of one's most intimate life companion. Grief embraces the full range of feelings that are generated by loss and unwanted change. The following list includes examples of the kinds of losses that can be expected to lead to upset.

Death: the loss of a loved one,
             friend, pet, etc.

Depression: the loss of hope

Divorce: the loss of a spouse, a
             relationship, a shared
             history, a lifestyle

Illness: the loss of health

Retirement: the loss of the focus of one's
             productivity

Moving: the loss of a home, roots, friends,
             neighborhood

Aging: the loss of health, physical
             appearance, strength, some
             competencies, etc.

Dealing with people who are experiencing the pain of a loss can be very stressful. Not only do we not know how to act or what to say, but we are afraid that we will say or do the wrong thing and make the other person's upset even greater. We erroneously think we should be able to make the upset person feel better, when, in fact, our primary task is to provide comfort.

In addition to our feelings of inadequacy, we may also experience feelings of vulnerability when faced with the upset person who is grieving.

> After the death of a five year-old child to leukemia, members of the community not only grieved over the loss, but also   identified with the pain in the death of a child, secretly harbored fears for their own children's health and safety, and experienced feelings of relief that this tragedy belonged to someone else.

Such a boiling cauldron of feelings obviously has an impact upon our ability to handle grief and upset.

Before discussing the appropriate behaviors for dealing with people who are upset over loss, it is first necessary to understand what is happening to them. Losing something, as we all know, is painful. Losing something hurts. Losing something creates a variety of feelings — feelings of varying hues, shades and intensities. Yet, despite the range of feelings, people who are grieving experience a predictable sequence of emotions and behaviors.

A number of people have written about this predictable grieving process, most notably Elizabeth Kubler-Ross. Kubler-Ross identifies five stages to the grief process. We have incorporated Kubler-Ross' and other theories and techniques into our counseling practice. Through the years, we have developed our own specific ideas about grief work as we have counseled with those who are trying to cope with difficult and painful life changes. We have applied grief counseling to a broad range of "loss" or "change" problems such as divorce, empty nest syndrome, illness, aging, etc. We'd like to share with you our specific ideas for successfully dealing with upset people who are grieving over loss or change.

THE RESPONSE CYCLE TO LOSS AND UNWANTED CHANGE

There are at least six predictable responses to loss and unwanted change. Once we can identify where in the response cycle the upset person is, we can tailor our own behavior to best help him or her.

A vivid childhood memory illustrates the first phase in the response to loss cycle. I (Pennie) was only four years old the day my mother bundled me up and raced with me over to my aunt's house. My aunt had just received a telegram stating that her nineteen year-old son, her only child, was missing in action in WW II. What bewildered the child in me was my aunt's behavior. I knew "her little boy" might be dead and yet she was playing the role of the impeccable hostess — welcoming 'the family and guests, rushing around the kitchen preparing food — in fact behaving quite normally. The only clue that gave away her numbness to the telegram was a large cut on her leg; the result of banging into the corner of a cabinet. The cut was bleeding profusely, yet obviously unfelt by her. When I asked my mother about this she said, "Aunt Claire can't feel her cut just like she can't feel her sadness. She hasn't really taken in the news yet."

Aunt Claire's reaction (or perhaps we should say her lack of reaction) typifies the initial response to any painful loss: *denial.* A large part of us is screaming, "Say it isn't so, this is not happening to me." The length of time a person in a grieving state denies his or her loss varies. In exteme cases people have been known to "pretend" forever that some particular life event never happened. More typically, the denial phase lasts just long enough for upset people to gather their strength and mobilize in order to deal with their loss. Denial is an early coping mechanism that helps people deal with their loss. It is useful to remember this in our contacts with those in mourning.

People in the denial phase of the grief cycle are not ready to accept their loss. In this phase, listening is especially important. Don't try to convince people of the reality of their loss. Do, however, quietly and calmly reiterate their situation. For example, to the grief-struck widow who is saying, "He just can't be gone. I can't believe he's dead," we don't say, "Harriet, you know Wesley is dead. You must accept this and come to terms with it." It is more helpful to say, "I understand how much you wish that Wesley was still alive. I know that you can hardly believe he's gone."

Only in cases where the grieving person continues to deny reality beyond a reasonable length of time might we consider some strategies for helping him or her to progress beyond denial. A reasonable length of time is, of course, often a matter of judgment. If we sense that denial is becoming either a lack of desire to face reality or a significant distortion of reality, this may indicate the upset person has exceeded normal limits for the denial phase. In such cases, gentle prodding, continuing reminders, and statements of concern are invaluable. "Harriet, Wes has been dead for several weeks now. I'm worried that you seem unable to accept this." Or, "Harriet, it concerns me that you are still acting as if Wes were alive. What would help you to come to terms with his death?" When denial becomes a loss of touch with reality, referral for professional help is recommended.

A second response to loss/grief/unwanted change is *anger.* People want to blame someone or something for the bad things that happen. When a loved one dies, anger may be directed at God, at doctors, at the hospital. When a job is lost, anger may be focused on the company, at the government. When a child fails in school, anger may be directed at the child's friends, teachers, or the school system. When a close friend moves away, we may be angry at the friend for leaving us. Examples of typical remarks from people in the anger phase of grief include: "It's not fair!" "The doctors don't know what they are doing." "It's all his (or her) fault." "You have no right to expect this of me."

The anger in grief is necessary and expectable. It is critical to understand that people who are hurting can express their hurt by being angry. We have a responsibility to deal with their hurt rather than their anger. Most of us can see beneath the anger to the hurt and anguish of the person grieving over a death. For example, we know intuitively that the man whose wife was just killed in an accident is screaming with rage because of the pain of his loss. There are other times, however, when this may be less clear. Let's imagine that a close friend has just been fired. After leaving the job in disbelief, he or she begins telling us how unfair and what a horrible person the boss is. All of this may be expressed quite angrily. If we are not careful, we can easily fall into the trap of reacting to the anger rather than to the loss.

Anger is a necessary and expectable part of the grief process. The angry person, of course, also needs a good listener. Be careful not to argue with the anger. Sometimes, well-intentioned friends and comforters struggle with their own religious or moral values when confronted by a person who is expressing anger over his or her loss. We may feel it isn't "right" for a person to be angry at God, at someone who is dead, or at the doctor. We need to stifle any reflexes we have that convey to the upset person that he or she shouldn't be angry. Rather, we need to give permission for the anger. "I can understand your anger." "I'd be angry too if I were left alone with three young children to care for." "Your rage at God is understandable." "You must feel so angry about how little Katherine has suffered."

It is useful to allow the angry person his or her anger for several reasons. For one thing, it keeps us from feeling frustrated when we are ineffective at changing another's behavior. We can't make other people's anger disappear.   And, paradoxically, granting people permission to be angry often results in their relinquishing the feeling. They feel understood!

Angry feelings that persist too long can impede the healing process and keep people from getting on with life. If we find the upset person maintaining an unhealthy anger for too long, referral to a professional may be in order. It may also be a time to be more confrontive.

> Vera resisted her divorce with all her strength. Her husband, Harry, was determined to get out of the marriage. Once divorce was inevitable, Vera's anger smoldered and eventually raged. At first her friends thought it was good for her to rant and rave about Harry. Six months later, they were getting tired of hearing the same angry war stories over and over again. Vera began demanding that none of her friends talk to Harry or see him socially. Anyone who invited Harry to dinner became her enemy. Finally, her closest friend, Gerry, said, "Vera, I think you need to come to terms with this anger at Harry. I'm getting weary of listening to you and I suspect others are, too. I know you don't want to drive your friends away. And I know you don't want to live this way forever, harboring such hateful feelings. If you can't do it alone, how about making an appointment with your minister or a counselor and trying to work out your feelings about the divorce?"

Once people begin to adjust to their loss, self-talk (as described in Chapter Three) changes from "this can't be happening" toward a more rational self-talk aimed at reducing the negative feelings. During this phase, called the *bargaining* or *accommodating* phase, the upset person may begin to express regret, may try to make sense of the situation, and/or may express a wish to have behaved differently in the past. Again, this is to be expected. "If only we had not had that argument." "If only I had gone to the hospital the night she died." "If God would only give me a chance to try again to be a better friend." "Well at least I won't experience more serious complications from this disease." "Thank God I only have diabetes instead of cancer."

These are the kinds of statements that can be expected from the person in the bargaining or accommodating phase. As you can see, upset people are looking for something positive in their loss. A congregation grieving over the upcoming departure of a beloved minister may refocus its grief onto some of the minister's qualities it won't miss. "Well, at least we won't have to put up with his messy study after he's gone" or "Let's hope our next minister has a better speaking voice." The divorcing wife may say, "I'll be glad not to have to listen to his snoring every night." It is healthy for bereaved people to look for the good in the bad. This is a sign that they are beginning to adjust to the loss. Bargaining and rationalizing help the upset person to adjust.

During the accommodating phase of the grief cycle, as upset people express regret and try to make sense of their situation, we can help them in several ways. As always, of course, we can listen and understand. "I know that you wish you had gone to the hospital the night Alice was so sick." "I know you wish you hadn't been unfaithful." "Retirement must be so difficult after so many years of an active work life." Statements of this type are appropriate. In addition, it is helpful to reassure the upset person. Reassurances need to fit the reality of the situation. They need to be "on target." "You did the best you were able to do at the time." "I would guess your wife would have understood that you needed to get some sleep that night." "You must have tried very hard to be a good employee."

Clarifying questions also serve a useful function for the upset person as he or she attempts to make sense of the loss. "Anything else you wish you would have said or done?" "What do you wish you had done differently?"   "What are some of your memories of Alice?" "Do you feel like you've learned something in this process?" "If your mother was here now, what do you think she'd say to you?"

All of these clarifying questions not only help the bereft person to understand his or her own situation, but they also give the person an opportunity to share feelings and ideas.

At some point *mourning* and *depression* is inevitable. The sense of loss brings sadness, a loss of energy, and a painful reflection on those things that will be missed. Bereft people often express that they are "just going through the motions." They may express feeling weary and exhausted. "I just don't have any energy. " "I feel helpless." "I am so lonely." "I miss being healthy."

Mourning and depression are necessary if people are going to survive loss. It is natural to feel sad when you have lost something. All religions, in their wisdom, allow for a formalized grieving process, recognizing its value in healing the wounds of loss. Depression and mourning are coping skills for dealing with loss. It would be a statement of our lack of humanness if we were not saddened by loss.

It is difficult for many of us to deal with the upset person who is depressed. We don't like to see people unhappy. We have to fight our natural tendency to want to make the other person feel better. The grieving person does not feel better by being told to "cheer up." He or she will feel better only as the wounds heal. The guidelines for handling depression in others are brief. Be there for the depressed person! Listen! Understand! Don't say much! Comfort, support, and permission to feel sad are what the person needs.

Most of us are more comfortable dealing with people in the final two stages of loss. The more difficult stages of denying, being angry, accommodating, and mourning are refreshingly followed by acceptance about loss. Life goes on and people begin to refocus on the present and the future and to revise their expectations to fit the reality of the situation. People who have begun to accept their situation express some hopefulness about the future. In this phase, we often hear people saying things like: "Well, I guess I'd better get on with my life." " I don't like what happened but I guess I'll have to live with it." "My diabetes is a nuisance, but it's not as bad as some illnesses."

As upset people begin to *accept* their sorrow or loss, *our* task is to shift gears with them. We need to be able to join them in their recovery process. Our primary goal in dealing with people who are in the acceptance phase is to encourage their acceptance. We can accomplish this through our appropriate behavior on Channels One, Two, and Three and by staying out of their way. As those we have been helping to accept their loss progress, we may need help in understanding that things change.

Maria had been very close to her mother who had died six months earlier. Her own grieving process had been somewhat aborted because her father had needed her support for his own overwhelming feelings of loss. After several months, her father met an attractive widow and, as might be expected, he began feeling better. Soon he was dating this woman and taking an active interest in life again. As her father accepted his loss and began to move on to revitalize, Maria was the one having difficulty coping with the death of her mother. It was hard for her to understand her father's recovery. Maria had not completed her own grieving. She resented his new companion not only for replacing her dead mother but also for replacing her as the primary caretaker of her father. Maria missed her mother and she also missed caring for her father.

Maria's father moved on and began planning a life after the death of his wife. It would be important for Maria not to share her own grief with her father if he was to continue to heal. But Maria now is faced with her own sense of loss. She could, of course, benefit from the patient and kindly ear of her family, a friend, a minister, or a counselor.

Acceptance of a loss sometimes blossoms into a complete *revitalization*.   Two years after Mary's husband left her, she had lost forty pounds, completed her college degree, embarked on a career with a pharmaceutical firm, and become the director of her church's choir. Mary developed a whole new sense of herself once she worked her way through the loss cycle. She was surging with a vitality and energy she hadn't experienced in years. Jim's wife had suffered with an illness for several years. Jim had been intimately involved in her care. He had much adjusting to do after her death. The bulk of his time and energy had been consumed by his wife's needs. Once the grieving process had been accomplished, Jim was surprised by his new-found energy and his sudden focus on planning for the future. All the energy that had gone into the care of his wife could now be redirected into new activities. Jim learned to play bridge, joined a health club, and became active in his church's singles' group. Once he accepted his wife's death, he was able to get on with his life.

In the revitalization phase, the previously upset person may develop new friends, new activities, new interests, and a new mate.   Acceptance and revitalization require our encouragement of the other person's development. As the grieving person resolves his or her painful feelings, we may, like Maria in the above illustration, be just beginning to experience our own feelings of loss. As situations change, friends may change. Retirees may no longer have much in common with old work friends. Widowed and divorced people may give up married friends and seek new single acquaintances. It is important to remember that we are not being rejected if this happens. Rather, it is a sign of the resolution of grief for the other person.

All of the six responses to loss are normal and necessary.   There is no exact length of time that is appropriate for each of the phases. Sometimes they don't follow in order.   Sometimes they overlap. Sometimes a response will reappear when least expected.

The Youngs had given birth to a severely retarded child in 1974. Following their doctor's advice, which was based on the severity of the child's handicap, the Youngs placed their daughter in an institutional setting. Their grief had been overwhelming. Eventually, however, they accepted their loss and out of it developed a great satisfaction from their volunteer work with the local Retarded Children's Association. Despite their long-term acceptance, Mr. & Mrs. Young continue to relive old emotions from time to time. Occasionally, anger and depression return to haunt them briefly.

Three Factors that Affect the Experience of Loss

Denial, anger, accommodation, mourning, acceptance, and revitalization each serve a function in helping people cope with loss or an unwanted change. Despite this predictable response cycle to grief, each person handles grief in his or her own individual way. The grief cycle varies in intensity and duration for different people. Some people cope with their sadness by crying; others by silence; others by talking; still others by listening to music.

When we are dealing with people upset over a loss, it behooves us to make a rough assessment about their ability to cope with their situation. Just as people differ in how they express grief, so, too, they differ in

the variety and strength of their *coping mechanisms.*
Obviously the greater the number and the strength of
these coping mechanisms, the more quickly the upset
person is likely to recover from a loss experience. For
example, the person with sound judgment, good
problem-solving skills, and quick reflexes will be better
able to restructure life if a fire destroys his or her home
than will a person without these skills. Similarly the
optimistic individual, who talks positively and rationally
to himself or herself, has better odds of bouncing back
after a loved one's death than the perennial pessimist.

In addition to assessing the upset person's coping
skills, we need to answer two questions, if we are to be
as helpful as possible. The first question is: "What is
the upset person's *perception* of his or her problem?"
To illustrate the importance of perception, let's look at
how two women, Jean and Chris, each viewed her
own situation after a divorce. Neither woman wanted a
divorce. Jean believed that if you weren't part of a
couple, you had no real place in the world. Her
previous identity as Mrs. James Fargo had been the
source of her self-esteem. Without a husband, she felt
she had little or no value. Chris, on the other hand,
believed that while spouses' lives are intertwined,

each person is an individual in his or her own right. She had a strong sense of who she was and did not believe that without a husband she was "nothing". She could not imagine her friends rejecting her because she had gotten a divorce. These differing perceptions about being single would greatly influence how each woman reacted to an unwanted divorce. Once we understand the perceptions each woman brings to her situation, we can have a clearer sense of how most appropriately to behave with each of them. Jean would probably need reassurance that she is acceptable and accepted. It would be very important to include her in couples' events, church gatherings, and so forth.   She might also profit from some help in developing new interests that would enhance her sense of competency and self-worth. Chris, on the other hand, might enjoy the opportunity to expand her already well-developed sense of herself as complete without a husband. A long, leisurely, chatty dinner with one or two close friends in addition to inclusion in church and social gatherings might be just what the doctor ordered. Chris might already be planning to join the church's singles' group, whereas Jean needs to be reassured that she still has her place with her coupled friends. Jean might need someone to offer her a ride to church; Chris might be offended if she feels her friends see her as unable to care for herself. The task is to match our responses to the upset person's perception of the dilemma while helping him or her to develop new perceptions as necessary. Ridicule in the form of, "Don't be silly. You're certainly old enough to take care of yourself, " or moralizing with statements such as, "You really should be mature enough to go to church alone on Sunday" is never helpful. The best way to help people develop new perceptions and new skills is through support and encouragement.

The final question to ask ourselves as we approach an upset grieving person relates to *support systems.*   Who or what can this person turn to for comfort and help? Does the upset person have friends, belong to clubs, have a church group, get along with the minister, have family, enjoy his or her job, etc? The more comfort and support one has during painful times, the better. How we respond to an upset grief-stricken person would depend, in part, on what we know about his or her support system. Picture the busy minister who has just learned that two of his congregants have suffered a traumatic loss.   This minister might appropriately choose   to allocate more time to the friendless, retired widow whose only child lives out of town than to the married, busy mother of three children who has the support of many people in the community. In such a case, it would be clear who had the most need for support. Not only might the widow profit from attention, but the busy mother might need some time to be alone with her grief.

Loss And Transactional Analysis

Transactional analysis was first discussed in Chapter Three. Throughout the book, we have used ideas from T.A. as a framework for understanding and dealing with upset people. T.A. concepts can be applied to dealing with loss and unwanted change in two ways. First of all, the same basic T.A. rules exist for dealing with people experiencing a loss as for dealing with complaining or angry people. People who are grief-stricken are behaving out of their child ego state. The child, as you recall, is the repository of all feelings, and grief is a feeling state. The ego states that most apply to our handling of bereavement are the caring parent and the adult. Those who have incurred a loss need comfort, which resides in the domain of the caring parent. Occasionally, our rational adult state may be needed to help upset people respond to problems that result from loss, but only after we have first provided comfort. The child within us can be helpful to the upset, bereaved person. It can be quite appropriate to cry with a dear friend whose child has just died or to be sad with an elderly person who is expressing pain about watching friends die. Sharing poignant feelings together can be comforting. As has been reiterated throughout the book, there is no place for the critical parent in dealing with upset.

There is a second way in which T.A. can be a useful tool as we learn to cope with those who are saddened. Until now, we have talked as if all losses are similar and, indeed, in many ways they are. There are, however, some ways in which losses differ from one another. These differences are more often in nature than in intensity. T.A. principles help us understand how losses differ from one another and how we might respond to different kinds of loss. Some losses are reality based. The loss of a loved one, being fired, losing your farm or business in a bankruptcy are all real losses. Conceptually, we might classify these real losses as belonging to the "adult."

Margaret sought psychiatric help after the death of her daughter because she felt she was not recovering properly. When she told the psychiatrist that she was severely depressed over this death, he responded: "This is a different kind of case for me. Losing your child is so real. Most other people I see are depressed and have no real reason for it."

Other losses belong to the "child." "Child" losses are less tangible. Nothing "real" has vanished and yet people still feel bereft, sad, and grief-stricken. The death of a wish, a dream, a hope, or a goal is such a loss. Often as we talk to men and women who are getting close to retirement, they express feelings of loss either because they have not reached life goals that they had established for themselves or because all of their goals have been realized and they are feeling as if they have nothing left to which to look foward.

A school music teacher augmented his income by giving trumpet lessons to beginning students. We learned in talking to him that he had graduated from the Julliard School of Music. His talent had been praised and he had expected an international concert career. His life didn't turn out that way. After a number of unsuccessful attempts to break into professional music, he returned to the Midwest. Still unable to make it in the local musical community, he took a job as an instrumental music teacher. Teaching eight-year-old beginning students, many of whom had little or no musical talent, was light years away from Carnegie Hall. This man was feeling lost and depressed — his hopes and dreams dashed.

While the loss of a dream is not as tangible as the loss of a loved one or the loss of a job, it can be, nevertheless, every bit as painful. It is important to be respectful of the mournful and depressed feelings of those who are saddened by the loss of wishes, dreams, and hopes.

People can also experience "parent" losses. A loss of faith, a loss of belief, and a loss of values are examples of "parent" losses. For example, growing up involves some loss for all of us. It is often depressing when we first learn that our minister, a beloved teacher, or our parents have human weaknesses. Many parent-child conflicts involve the parents' difficulty in adjusting to a loss. We usually call this kind of loss "coping with a changing world." Our grandparents or parents may have walked to school, but today's teenagers rely on their "wheels." The open discussion of sex and sexuality may have been taboo fifty years ago, but that is no longer the case. Parents may mourn the loss of a simpler (or a different) lifestyle. They may wish that things would be more like they used to be.

Karen had allowed herself to have an extramarital affair with a man who had been a close friend for many years. She had held strong convictions about marital fidelity and was overwhelmed with feelings of guilt and shame. Her personal loss of a long-held value was painful to her. In addition to breaking off the affair, Karen had to grieve the temporary loss of an important value, of a belief in and about herself.

All three kinds of loss require comforting, caring, nurturing, listening, and being there. In addition, reality based losses usually forecast significant life changes to which people will need to adjust. These might include: "How am I going to spend my time now that my children are grown and out of the nest?" "How can I learn to handle my finances without Tony?" "How can I make a living now that I have lost my job?"

Child state losses of hopes and dreams are best served by quiet comforting. Since the loss of hopes, dreams, and wishes doesn't require an immediate adjustment in current life situation, a good ear and lots of understanding will usually do the trick. We can also use our personal knowledge of the grieving individual to redirect goals, hopes, and dreams.

A minister who came for counseling was feeling depressed as he approached retirement. Most of his career goals had been met. He felt he had nothing left to look foward to. During one of the counseling sessions, he described his life-long interest in history and how he had read widely about the Civil War and had been chewing on some important ideas he had at one time considered writing about. With a little encouragement, he slowly began changing his feelings about retirement. Freedom from regular work and from the pursuit of career goals would permit him valuable time in which he could put his ideas on paper.

Encouragement is not the same thing as pushing and prodding. Encouragement means creating an atmosphere through listening and understanding that gives the grieving person the freedom to explore new possibilities.

Parent state losses of faith, belief, or values also respond well to good listening skills. People struggling with loss of faith or belief are usually very hard on themselves. It is wise not to add to their burden by moralizing to them.

Applying the Seven Channels

Although I (Pennie) was only thirteen years old when my father died, I remember vividly my different responses to the various well-wishers who visited the house after the funeral. Some visitors talked incessantly, probably out of their own awkwardness. A few tried to talk me out of my grief by saying such things as "You should be glad he didn't suffer," "You should be pleased God wanted to call him home," "Your father wouldn't want you to be sad," etc. And some permitted me to express my grief by reminiscing with me about my father, through their quiet acceptance of my grief, or by hugging me and letting me cry. This experience taught me, at an early age, what works best for the bereaved person — silence, understanding, and permission to express one's pain.

To reemphasize, listening and empathizing are the meat and potatoes of what we have to say about dealing with those who are upset because of loss. It is necessary, however, to garnish the main course by discussing specific behaviors to which grieving people respond well. Let's begin by looking at how we might use each of the seven channels of communication to handle upset generated by grief, loss, or unwanted change.

Each of the channels of communication has the potential to help or hinder the grieving process. Strange as it may sound, the most helpful message to send to the sad, upset person on *Channel One*, the language channel, is no message at all. Silence is truly golden to the distressed, bereaved person. Quietly sharing the pain, the tears, or the sadness is poignant and comforting to those experiencing sorrow. There is no need to think of the "right" thing to say in a house of mourning (what a relief!). All you have to do is let the bereaved person know you are there and that you care. Your presence and your attention send this message loud and clear. Since upset people may need to express their feelings, good listening skills are far more important than having a "way with words."

Channel Two, the manner channel, and *Channel Three*, body language, help to carry the message of caring to the upset person. Physical closeness and touching can be powerful healers. A hug, a pat on the shoulder, a lingering handshake, or a caring look all convey the important message of "I'm here and I care" to the suffering person. Match the level of your behavior on Channels Two and Three to fit the person's loss, the intimacy of your relationship, and the cues that you receive from the bereaved. Approaching a business acquaintance who has just lost her job will involve a simple handshake and "I'm sorry about the job." On the other hand, when an intimate friend experiences a significant loss, you will no doubt be on his or her doorstep within minutes and will use more intimate nonverbal behaviors to announce that it is all right to let down. The relief for the upset person can be enormous!

As you observe people who are dealing with a loss, you may notice many different feelings being expressed on *Channel Four*. It is not unusual for there to be feelings of numbness — times when feelings are repressed. Relief and happiness may even be experienced.

> Not long ago a woman expressed to us a bewildering potpourri of feelings. It had been her habit to call her mother every Saturday morning. For several months after her mother's death, she would awaken on Saturdays feeling happy and anticipatory about talking to her mother. When the reality of her mother's death sunk in, she would seesaw into the depths of depression.

Upset may be demonstrated in a variety of ways. Whatever the feelings of upset people and whatever the style they employ to express those feelings, it is important to give permission for the person to have the feelings. Whether it be screaming, sobbing, silence, quiet tears, nervous laughter, or constant chattering, we only need let it be. People have individual ways of letting their feelings out and their own time schedules for this release.

As for what you do with your own feelings during

these times, we offer several suggestions. Very upset people often need the reassurance that someone is in control. Therefore, when possible, try to convey quiet strength and control. There are times, of course, when this is neither possible nor necessary. Our feelings may be intimately affected by our own involvement with the loss. When our closest friends are upset because they have just learned that the family will be moving across the country, we are also upset. Their move is our loss, too. In this case it is expected and appropriate to grieve together. But if a friend's mother whom we barely knew dies, our own feelings are not significantly involved. We can honestly turn most of our attention toward caring for our grieving friend. Try to match your emotional tone to the requirements of the situation. Your personal feelings of inadequacy and vulnerability mentioned at the beginning of this chapter are natural, but may need to be monitored. While it can be perfectly appropriate to say "I feel so inadequate at a time like this," it is not appropriate to *maintain* the spotlight on your own feelings. You may also find that you have to monitor feelings of irritation with the upset person. You may feel that they are grieving too "long" or too "strong." If you cannot talk to yourself about your own feelings in a way that helps your attitudes and your behaviors, it might be wise to back away from the situation for a time.

We have a powerful opportunity to provide comfort and consolation on *Channel Five*, the symbolic communication channel. It is often the small symbolic gestures that smooth pain and mean a lot. Phone calls, notes, or visits to the elderly, to those who are weeks or months beyond the death of a loved one, or to the housebound mean a great deal. Bringing food to the house of mourning, writing down a phone number for an upset friend, driving an elderly person to a church meeting all provide significant support.

All of our lives are busy. None of us can minister to everyone. But each of us has the time to make a few symbolic gestures to someone in need. If we can be selective and not take on more than we can comfortably handle, the opportunity to make an impact is available. Think in small but meaningful terms. We may be able to bake a pie or fix a leaky faucet for the friend in need, but preparing a three-course dinner for a family of eight or remodeling the neighbor's kitchen would burden us beyond our resources. The goal is to be helpful, not an angry and resentful martyr. One value of symbolic communication is that it reminds us that more often it is the "thought that counts" not the magnitude of the gesture.

Channel Six, territory, involves some special application when dealing with loss and the upset that surrounds it. When people are complaining or angry, the last thing we want to do is violate their personal or psychological territory. But at times of bereavement, people often want and need intimacy. It is precisely at times of loss and grief that our social norms permit and even encourage the letting down of barriers that sometimes hinder closeness. Holding a grieving friend can provide much needed solace. Even a gentle touch on the shoulder or arm can imply a tender ministering. Once again, it is important to match the intimate use of territory to the occasion and to the relationship. While hugging a close friend who is experiencing profound loss may be comforting, hugging the casual acquaintance who has recently retired will more likely add to his or her discomfort.

Psychologically as well as physically, grieving people are usually more responsive to sharing intimately than angry, upset people.

A friend who was going through a painful divorce from his wife of thirty years had announced that he didn't want to talk about it with anyone. However, when I (Don) asked him to have lunch, it was only a matter of minutes before he freely began sharing some of the pain he was experiencing.

While not pushing my friend to share, I did intrude slightly into his intimate psychological zone by saying that I was sorry to hear about his divorce and if there was anything I could do to be helpful, I wanted him to know I was there to help. By carefully reading people on Channels Two and Three, we can more naturally match our territorial position to their preferences. It is through their manner and their body language that upset people say "come on in" or "back off."

As in any kind of upset, our behavior, *Channel Seven*, influences people who are experiencing a loss. It is what we do, in addition to what we say, that counts. Phone calls, visits, letters, cooking for a bereaved family, watching the child of a sick friend, or providing a meal to the family in the midst of a financial crisis are more than symbolic gestures. They are also intentional actions that count for a lot. Gestures don't need to be big ones. They should, however, fill a need for the person who is experiencing the loss. Behaviors that best help upset people are actions that are helpful

without being intrusive. Putting ourselves in the other
person's shoes assists in finding this delicate balance.
Asking ourselves "What would I want and/or need if my
spouse had just died?" or "What would I appreciate if I
were elderly, handicapped, and without family?" are
the kinds of questions that result in appropriate
behavior.

In summary,   the   seven   channels   of
communication provide a framework for dealing with
upset people who are coping with the pain of loss or
unwanted change. Silence, appropriate verbal and
nonverbal expression of understanding and sympathy,
and symbolic and tangible gestures of your caring are
the keys to successful handling.

The Formula and Practice

The basic formula for dealing with upset persons
is as applicable to dealing with grief as it is to dealing
with the upset generated by complaints and anger.
Listening, empathizing, clarifying, problem solving,
and *closing* are each a part of the process. There are,
however, some unique timing issues related to dealing
with those in grief. Whereas we can hope to resolve
complaining or angry upset quickly, this is not so when

it comes to upset created by loss or unwanted change. Time truly is a healer. Therefore, each of us needs to be patient as we work with the upset, bereaved person. As always, remember to use your caring parent state first, and then only if necessary, your rational adult state. Apply the channels of communication to the formula as suggested. Be aware of the kind of loss the upset person is experiencing and where the person is in the grief process.   We believe that if you put all of this to work, not only will the upset person benefit, but you, too, will find the difficult task of comforting those in pain less frightening.

Practice is, as always, helpful. In this case, however, we realize that it is a bit macabre to plan what you will say and do if some tragedy should befall someone you know. What you can do, however, is remember some tough spots in which you have found yourself in the past. Try to remember not only what you did at the time but what effect it had on the upset people. Then, replay some of those experiences, imagining yourself using the suggestions presented in this chapter. In the future, when you have to deal with a difficult loss situation, allow yourself a few moments to review this chapter. When time permits, rehearse in your head what you might say and do. Be sure to remind yourself that, for the most part, little is expected from you. If you truly care, all you have to do is be there and let it show.

And Finally . . .

Before closing this chapter, there are three final suggestions we'd like to make. The first of these relates to the use of humor in dealing with upset people. Upset, particularly the upset generated by loss and bereavement, can make us "deadly" serious. Sometimes, a lighter touch is needed to relieve the tension. The value of humor was observed when we attended a friend's funeral last year. After the service, as friends and family were gathered together, laughter reverberated amid much reminiscing and joking. Suddenly, one of the guests said, "This is awful. Here we are laughing and carrying on at a funeral." Another guest offered, "I think this is great. No one liked a good party more than Fred did. In case you can hear us, Fred, this joke's for you." The appropriate use of humor can be an excellent healer.

As we mentioned earlier, referral is a necessary and valuable tool. We'd like to underline at this point that   if you feel in over your head, referral is an excellent option. Referral may be helpful in providing distance from upset in which you are too emotionally involved. A good referral implies helpfulness. You are suggesting someone (another friend, relative, minister, counselor, etc.) who you think can help the upset person better than you can. Referral is not failure. It is good common sense.

Finally, keep in mind that grieving people also can be needy people who unintentionally deplete our reserves. We need to take care of ourselves while caring for others. It is not surprising that many ministers and other helping professionals find their way into our counseling offices. Often, the   problem is one of exhaustion — physical and emotional. The demands of other people can lead to fatigue. It is wise to know your limits; selectively choose when and where to help; and at times assertively say "no." All of our resources are finite. When we are emotionally drained, we cannot be helpful to anyone. This is a reminder to nourish and care for yourself while you are ministering to others.

CHAPTER EIGHT
PUTTING IT ALL TOGETHER

He might have been considered a "young" minister in terms of his age and the number of years he had headed a congregation. But the members of his church saw him as a man of wisdom and compassion far beyond his years. Almost to a person, his congregants turned to him in their hours of need. When queried as to the secret of his success in a role that frequently brings nothing but criticism, one congregant replied: "He is real, not a phony; usually pleasant and good natured. He tries to get to know us. He listens, and he understands. He never seems to judge us. He rarely lectures us or gives us advice. But somehow when all is said and done, we seem not only to feel better but also to have a better understanding of ourselves and our problems."

This story about a young minister in a small Kansas town illustrates beautifully what dealing with people is all about. The ideas discussed in this book are anchored in good old-fashioned common sense. None of the principles, formulas, or strategies for handling upset people is very complicated. Yet, at times all of us find dealing with upset persons a challenging task.

We began Chapter One by asking you to take the

208

Dealing With Upset Persons Profile. Before reading any further, we would ask you to review the Profile found on pages six and seven, retaking it if you wish.

Of course, by now you know that the responses to the statements which lead to the best handling of upset people are numbers 4 and 5. The Profile was not designed to be complicated or tricky but rather to reinforce attitudes and behaviors that will be useful to you as you find yourself confronted with people upset over a variety of issues and problems. Each statement on the Profile addresses an important point related to dealing with upset persons. All of these concepts have been discussed in the book.

At this time we would like to restate the items on the Profile in a manner that highlights and summarizes the basic principles for *Dealing With Upset Persons.*

1)   *Listen.* Good listening skills are the single most important tool for dealing with people who are upset. Being able to air feelings has prevented or cured a world of upset.

> My (Pennie's) son is on the threshold of young adulthood; a time when one is easily upset because of all the life decisions waiting to be confronted. One of his recent long-distance calls   revealed a   moderate degree of upset over some career decisions that he needed to

make. Like all parents, I had some ideas and opinions about his situation. Biting my tongue, I chose instead to say, "I'm not going to give you any advice. I love you very much and will support you in whatever decision you make. Can you share some of your own thinking as it pertains to this decision?" Not to my surprise, he proceeded to talk about his career concerns in a way that indicated he was aware of those issues that I wanted to be sure he was examining. He and I shared many of the same ideas and opinions, worries, fears, and hopes. In his process of "talking it out," he began to see more clearly which path to take. My role needed to be only one of being an "ear."

2) *Empathize.*   There are two critical points to reiterate here. The first is a reminder of the importance of empathy — of being able to put oneself in another's shoes. Empathy, like listening, is an invaluable aid for defusing upset. The second is remembering that to understand is not to take responsibility. You can show concern and understanding without assuming liability. There is no need to hold back our understanding out of the fear of becoming responsible.

3) *Set the tone.* In our conversations with others, we have some responsibility for setting a tone or mood that is positive. If we let others set the tone, we are giving them too much power and control over us. Positive contact is critical to the prevention of upset. We will

experience greater success in our relationships with others if the tone we set is a positive one.

4) *Caring parents and adults.* Calming upset people requires two basic behaviors from us: caring and rationality.   We comfort upset people by behaving as caring parents (described in Chapter Three, the Transactional Analysis Model). If the upset person has a problem that needs solving, we then use our rational adult state. The critical person who convinces, lectures, or moralizes is *not* successful with upset people.

5) *Focus your attention on others — particularly when they are upset.* Most people prefer to talk about themselves rather than to listen to others, especially when they are upset. That's why listening is such a valuable skill. Good listeners allow others to talk. It is impossible to listen well while talking.

6) *People require attention.* Positive contact involves attending to others in a timely fashion. This avoids the secondary upset that results when people feel ignored. If people are already upset, having to wait for our attention adds to the strength of their upset feelings.

7) *No one is expected to have all the answers.* Being helpful doesn't mean having solutions or being a smooth talker.

8) *Upset people need to share their upset.* There is a strong need to air negative feeelings when people are upset. The ventilation of upset is similar to the steam release valve on a pressure cooker. The release of steam prevents the cooker from exploding. Upset people may feel as if they are going to explode unless they can release some of their feelings. Therefore, whether or not there are solutions to reduce the upsetting problem and whether or not we can be helpful in finding that solution, we can help upset people just by listening to the expression of the upset.

9) *Listen nondefensively for issues.* We need to avoid the natural tendency to defend ourselves when attacked by upset people. The best way not to feel personally attacked is to listen for the *issues* in the person's upset rather than to focus on those comments which appear to be blaming of us. If we can successfully focus our attention on the problem underlying the upset, we can help the other person to do likewise. And, if we can stay clear from feeling personally attacked, we are more likely to be able to maintain the helpful stances of a caring parent and a rational adult.

10) *Maintaining the goal of helpfulness.* The primary goal in dealing with upset people is to reduce their upset; to help them to feel better. The brilliance and/or wit of our own oratory is not a consideration. Helping others to feel better also helps us. It is valuable if all the parties to an upsetting situation can maintain their self-esteem.

11) *The art of good referral.* A good referral is a sign of success.

12) *People are responsible for themselves.* We will not always be able to help someone who is upset. Some upset people choose to maintain an angry, critical, complaining, or depressed stance. We can only do our best. We can't make people happy. Some problems can't be solved. All we can offer the upset person with such a problem is a good ear and lots of understanding.

Some Parting Ideas . . .

Before we end our book, we'd like to leave you on a more philosophical note. We know that dealing with upset can be a trying and painful process. Negative emotions are difficult to handle. Many of us were never taught any skills for handling either our own negative emotions or those of other people. Take a few moments to think about the ways in which it was permissible for you to be angry as a child. We have asked this question of many people over the years. A majority of those to whom we have posed this question realized that all behaviors related to being angry or upset were criticized and thwarted. One man said, "Come to think of it, I wasn't allowed to yell; I wasn't allowed to be silent; I wasn't supposed to pout; I wasn't to say things that weren't nice; I wasn't allowed to slam doors or stomp around; I wasn't allowed to be physically angry in any way; I wasn't supposed to cry; and I wasn't allowed to have a tantrum. I guess when I think about it, I just wasn't ever supposed to be angry."

Most of us learned as children to be careful not to say or do anything that would anger other people. The childhood fear of upsetting others makes sense when we realize how dependent children are on other people to get their needs met. It can be very scary to feel helpless and to fear that the people you need may refuse to help you if they are angry at you. As we mature and develop, however, we become less helpless. We become responsible for taking care of ourselves. We no longer have to be quite so frightened that upsetting others will have dire consequences for us. And yet, these old childhood fears remain.

> Recently, we received a call from a woman named Elinor who was quite upset. She had just learned about a genetic problem in her family; a problem that might have serious implications for as yet unborn children in the family. Elinor's daughter and son-in-law were beginning to think about having a family. She had wanted to tell them about the implications for them of the genetic problem but her husband had told her not to say anything. Elinor felt that it would not be "right" to stay silent. When asked what was keeping her from discussing the problem with her children, Elinor said, "I won't be able to live with myself if I don't tell my children about this, but I can't because my husband will be mad at me." After listening to Elinor's concerns, one of us asked with some intentional humor: "Will this be the first time your husband has ever been mad at you?" Elinor threw her head back and enjoyed a good laugh. "You've got a point there," she finally said. "I think I will have to do what *I* think is right. After all, it's me who has to live with me."

Elinor was responding as many of us do out of a mistaken idea that something catastrophic will happen if someone is upset with us. Anger, sadness, frustration, and despair do not forecast catastrophy. They are just human emotions. As adults, we need to develop some comfort with the ability to handle the full range of emotions in ourselves and others. It is our strong belief that while "sticks and stones may break our bones," upset feelings do not have to hurt us. This belief encouraged us to develop and teach our seminar and to write this book.

Not only isn't the expression of upset harmful, but it can have great value. We mentioned earlier in the book that people who complain and share their upset are providing necessary feedback. We have to know what's upsetting someone before we can work on the problem. People who are willing to share their upset are trying to stay involved with us. In our experience as marriage counselors we have learned that the couples least likely to work things out are those who are so resigned to failure that they have stopped talking and stopped fighting. To be upset together, angry together, and sad together is to care enough to share feelings and to care enough to put energy into trying to change things.

The expression of upset feelings can "clear the air." People can feel better after an explosion of upset, be it through crying, yelling, slamming a door, or taking a brisk walk. We need to remind ourselves that the expression of upset siphons off the steam.

While our primary goal is to prevent *unnecessary* upset in others through positive contact, some upset is necessary and/or inevitable. Consequently we have two important tasks to consider when dealing with those who are upset.

- how to handle our own feelings effectively
- how to deal with the upset person effectively

This book provides the formulas to assist you in these tasks. Let's quickly recap the general formula for dealing with upset persons.

- Listen
- Empathize
- Clarify
- Problem solve (if necessary)
- Close

The attitudes, behaviors, and principles discussed throughout this book will help you exchange your old anxious feelings for concrete skills for dealing with upset people. We are convinced that the more you develop an optimistic attitude about complaints and upset and the more you practice the behaviors we have described, the better you'll get at handling upset people. If your life is a typical one, you will no doubt have numerous opportunities to put our suggestions to work. There will always be upset people. You now have the knowledge both to prevent unnecessary upset and to deal with those who are already upset. We wish you success! You and those whom your life touches will be the beneficiaries.

REFERENCES AND READINGS

Ables, B.S. (1979). *Therapy for couples.* San Francisco: Jossey-Bass Publishers.

Alberti, R.E., & Emmons, M.L. (1975). *Stand up , speak out, talk back.* New York: Pocket Books.

Berne, E. (1967). *Games people play.* New York: Grove Press.

Berne, E. (1972). *What do you say after you say hello?* New York: Bantam Books.

Bernstein, L., Bernstein, A.S., & Dana, R. (1974). *Interviewing: A guide for health professionals.* New York: Appleton-Century-Crofts.

Bower, S.A. & Bower, G.H. (1972). *Asserting yourself.* Reading, Mass: Addison-Wesley Publishing Co.

Caine, L. (1974). *Widow.* New York: Bantam Books.

Carkhuff, R.R. (1969). *Helping and human relations.* New York: Holt, Rinehart & Winston, Inc.

DiMatteo, M. R., & DiNicola, D. D. (1982). *Achieving patient compliance.* New York: Pergammon Press.

Dreikurs, R. (1972). *The challenge of child training: A parents' guide.* New York: Hawthorn Books.

Drury, S. S. (1984). *Assertive supervision.* Champaign, Ill.: Reasearch Press.

Ellis, A. & Grieger, R. (1977). *RET Handbook of rational-emotive therapy.* New York: Springer Publishing Co.

Fournies, F. F. (1978). *Coaching for improved work performance.* New York: VanNostrand Reinhold Company.

Filley, A. C. (1975). *Interpersonal conflict resolution.* Glenview, Ill.: Scott, Foresman and Co.

Hallett, K. (1974). *A guide for single parents: Transactional analysis for people in crisis.* Millbrae, Ca.: Celestial Arts.

Harris, T. A. (1967). *I'm O.K.—You're O.K.* New York: Harper and Row.

James, M., & Jongeward, D. (1971). *Born to win.* Reading, Mass: Addison-Wesley.

Kübler-Ross, E. (1975). *Death the final stage of growth.* Englewood Cliffs, N.J.: Prentice-Hall.

Kübler-Ross, E. (1969). *On death and dying.* New York: Macmillan Publishing Co., Inc.

Lange, A.J., & Jakubowski, P. (1976). *Responsible assertive behavior.* Champaign, Ill: Research Press.

Ling, M. (1963). *How to increase sales and put yourself across by telephone.* Englewood Cliffs, N.J.: Prentice Hall.

Mahoney, M.J. (1979). *Self change: Strategies for solving personal problems.* New York: W.W. Norton.

Papp, P. (1983). *The process of change.* New York: Guilford Press.

Puryear, D. A. (1979). *Helping people in crisis.* San Francisco: Jossey-Bass Publishers.

Satir, V. (1972). *Peoplemaking.* Palo Alto, California: Science and Behavior Books, Inc.

Silverstone, B., & Hyman, H.(1976). *You and your aging parents.* New York: Pantheon.

Smith, M. J. (1975). *When I say no, I feel guilty.* New York: Bantam Books.

Spector, G. A. (1973). *Crisis intervention.* New York: Behavioral Publications.

Strayhorn, J. M. Jr. (1977). *Talking it out.* Champaign, Ill: Research Press.

Sundel, S. S., & Sundel, M. (1980). *Be assertive: A practical guide for human service workers.* Beverly Hills, Ca.: Sage Publications.

Tavris, C. (1982). *Anger.* New York: Simon and Shuster.

Universal Training Systems (1979). *Improving customer relations.* Wilmette, Ill.

Villerè, M. F. (1981). *Transactional analysis at work.* Englewood Cliffs, N.J.: Prentice-Hall.

Watzlawick, P., Weakland, J., & Fisch, R. (1974). *Change.* New York: W.W. Norton.

Zimbardo, P. (1977). *Shyness.* Reading, Mass: Addison-Wesley Publishing Co.

About the authors:

Pennie Myers Ed.D. is on the Counseling Center and Gerontology faculties of The Wichita State University. Trained in counseling and a clinical member and approved supervisor for the American Association for Marriage and Family Therapists, Myers has expanded her family systems orientation into working with larger groups in business, industry, and the professional community.

Don Nance, Ph.D. is Director of Counseling at The Wichita State University. Through his counseling, teaching and consulting, Nance has over twenty years experience working with people in a broad range of settings to manage a variety of problems. His ability to translate complex psychological principles into everyday language resulted in his being awarded his university's "Excellence In Teaching" award.

Myers and Nance have been a successful professional team for over ten years. In addition to their faculty positions, they are partners in Mid-America Consulting Services through which they have worked with a variety of clients including: church groups and volunteer organizations; school districts and local governments; small companies and large corporations. If you have an interest in presenting a program on Dealing With Upset People or providing other effective public contact skill training, contact the authors, c/o The Wichita State University, Wichita, Kansas, 67208-1595, (316) 689-3440.